CONTENTS: Introduction, 8; Getting Started, 24; Cages and Aviaries, 34; Feeding and Care, 42; Breeding, 56; Diseases, 64; Finch Species, 70

Front Covers: Diamond finch, *Zonaeginthus guttatus*. Photo: K. Hindwood.
Back Covers: 1. Star finch, *Balthilda ruficauda;*
2. Longtailed grass finch, *Poephila acuticauda;*
3. Cherry finch, *Aidemosyne modesta;*
4. Gouldian finch, *Chloebia gouldiae*

Photos: Horst Muller

Front endpapers: Gouldian finches. Photo by Harry V. Lacey.
Back endpapers: Zebra finches. Photo by Harry V. Lacey.

ISBN 0-87666-987-9 ● KW-027

Color Photos:
G. Ebben: 18 (1), 99 (5), 122 (3).
Keith Hindwood: 26 (3), 27 (5).
Harry V. Lacey: 2, 3, 7 (4, 5), 10 (1, 2, 3), 11 (5), 106 (3), 110 (3), 111 (5), 123 (5), 127.
Horst Muller: 6 (2), 11 (4), 14, 15 (4), 18 (3), 19 (4), 22 (1, 2), 23 (4), 26 (1, 2), 27 (4), 31, 98, 99 (4), 102, 103 (5), 106 (1, 2), 107 (4), 110 (1, 2), 111 (4), 114, 115, 118 (1, 2), 122 (1, 2), 123 (4).
Louise van der Meid: 6 (1), 10, 18 (2), 19 (5), 103.
Dr. Matthew M. Vriends: 22 (3), 23 (4), 107 (5), 118 (3).

Black and White Photos:
Al Barry: 25
Harry V. Lacey: 8-9, 21, 24, 34, 35, 41, 42, 56, 57, 63, 64, 65, 69, 70, 71, 125.
Louise van der Meid: 5, 43, 55.

Originally published in German by Franckh'sche Verlagshandlung, W. Keller & Co. Stuttgart/1975 under the title *Australische Prachtfinken*. First edition © 1975 by Franckh'sche Verlagshandlung.

Distributed in the U.S. by T.F.H. Publications, Inc., 211 West Sylvania Avenue, P.O. Box 427, Neptune, N.J. 07753; in England by T.F.H. (Gt. Britain) Ltd., 13 Nutley Lane, Reigate, Surrey; in Canada to the book store and library trade by Beaverbooks, 953 Dillingham Road, Pickering, Ontario L1W 1Z7; in Canada to the pet trade by Rolf C. Hagen Ltd., 3225 Sartelon Street, Montreal 382, Quebec; in Southeast Asia by Y.W. Ong, 9 Lorong 36 Geylang, Singapore 14; in Australia and the South Pacific by Pet Imports Pty. Ltd., P.O. Box 149, Brookvale 2100, N.S.W., Australia; in South Africa by Valiant Publishers (Pty.) Ltd., P.O. Box 78236, Sandton City, 2146, South Africa; Published by T.F.H. Publications, Inc., Ltd., The British Crown Colony of Hong Kong.

Australian Finches

CURT AF ENEHJELM

TRANSLATED BY U. ERICH FRIESE

Zebra finches adapt to all sorts of environments. They feed on half-ripe grass seeds and on some insects. In captivity they breed freely and are exceptionally peaceful when gregariously kept. 1 and 2, males; 3, pair, male above; 4, pair, male in foreground; 5, pair, female above.

4

5

Zebra finches incubate diligently and are seldom disturbed by periodical inspection of the nest. They become terribly fussy once the young birds have been hatched.

Introduction

8

The Australian grass finches are among the most popular cage birds, and as such they form a sizable segment of the bird market. Originally they were considered to be a subfamily of the weaver birds, but now they are grouped in their own family, Estrildidae (often referred to as weaver finches), which contains about 120 species and many subspecies. The grace and beauty of these birds, together with the fact that many will readily breed in captivity, have made them very popular as cage and aviary birds.

The natural distribution of estrildine finches extends from Africa (south of the Sahara Desert) to Madagascar and southern Arabia, northward towards southern China and

The zebra finch (1, 2, 3, 5) of Australia presents no problems. It is easy to house in aviaries and large cages. The species is quite domesticated and comes in a variety of colors. The cherry finch or plum-head finch (*Aidemosyne modesta*) (4) is quite aggressive during brooding and rearing the young.

4

5

Taiwan; they are also widespread throughout the Indo-Australian Archipelago, from the Australian mainland to Papua-New Guinea and eastward towards Micronesia and Samoa. They do not occur, however, in New Zealand. In addition, they have also been introduced to other countries which have a tropical or at least temperate climate, where they have often become well established. For instance, there is one species now even on the European continent (in Portugal).

This book will cover the so-called *grass finches* from Australia and the related *parrot finches* from the Indo-Pacific Islands. In appearance and body shape these birds resemble the related true finches as well as the weavers. However, they are distinguished from true finches, as well as from weavers and sparrows, by the presence of 10 primary wing feathers, as opposed to 9 in the true finches.

Many species are conspicuously colored in bright reds, greens, blues or yellows, while some are rather plain. Males and females can often be recognized on the basis of different color patterns. There is an equally large number though, in which there are no color differences whatsoever between the sexes.

Depending upon the species, the beak in grass finches is variably colored, mostly in shades of red, but often yellow, whitish, gray or metallic blue. It is either stout and thick or pointed and slender, again depending upon the individual species.

The tail varies in shape, form and length with most grass finches; it may be either rounded, serrated or truncated in a straight line. The central tail feathers are often pointed, and in two species they are extended and finely pointed.

Many of these finches show very characteristic tail movements. The grass finches often fan their tails impressively to the left and right. Others, such as the amarants, move their tails vertically up and down.

In size, grass finches range from about 9 cm (zebra finch)

to about 14 cm (crimson finch, *Neochmia phaeton*, and Gouldian finch, *Chloebia gouldiae*).

Many species live in savannah country, while others prefer dense jungle and still others live in the proximity of human habitation, such as within native villages or in city or town parks. A few inhabit mountainous regions up to considerable altitudes. Most of these finches stay close to the ground or remain within low bushes and some are distinctly ground dwellers.

Grass and parrot finches feed predominantly on ripe (dry) and half-ripe seeds, but they will also take on insects, particularly when they are rearing young. A few rarely imported species feed exclusively on insects, such as flying ants and termites, which are caught in flight. In general, these finches look for food on the ground and pick up seeds from various seed pods. Many are quite adept in clinging to grass reeds while picking seeds from the pods. Some Australian species sip water in the same manner pigeons do (zebra finch, diamond firetail finch, star finch, and masked finch). All others raise the beak, in a chicken-like manner, after each swallow.

Most grass finches are very social birds which live together in small or large groups. They exhibit a considerable degree of social behavior, such as maintaining body contact during mutual preening and when resting. Body contact is maintained either through long rows of birds sitting side by side or through individual pairs sitting side by side. Some species will not tolerate any intra-specific body contact and always maintain a certain distance between individual birds. The degree of body contact varies among the different species. The same holds true for mutual feather preening, whereby one bird picks on the head and neck feathers of another. Mutual preening is particularly strongly expressed by those species which have the greatest need for body contact. Unfortunately, in captivity such preening can intensify to a point at which the birds are pulling each

13

1

2

3

The long-tailed grass finch (1, 3, 4, 5) lives in the savannah and feeds on grass seeds; it is well suited to being kept in spacious aviaries during summertime. (2) is a female zebra finch.

4

5

other's feathers out. This was particularly noticeable during the early days when birds were imported by boat. On board ship the birds had to remain in overcrowded shipping boxes for prolonged periods of time. Nowadays, birds are transported by air, so this phenomenon rarely occurs.

During the breeding season most pairs build their nests in close proximity to each other, often in the same bush or tree. This behavior is fundamentally different from that of the true finches, which are strongly territorial even at the intra-specific level. Such total isolation occurs only rarely among grass and parrot finches; a notable exception is the rather aggressive crimson finch, *Neochmia phaeton*. This species not only drives off other crimson finches but also attacks much larger birds that invade its territory.

The call of the grass finches is generally very faint and often rather unmelodic. Unlike males of the species of true finches, which indicate their territory through their tone, grass finch males use the voice only during courtship. In some species the females too will vocalize. In addition to courting calls, these birds can produce a wide range of other sounds—attracting calls, which sometimes vary between the sexes in some species, warning or fright calls, attracting-to-nest calls and others.

Most grass and parrot finches are very peaceful. Courtship behavior varies among species, but usually the male performs a ritualistic courtship dance. During this dance he either sings and dances directly in front of or towards the female, or he dances a semi-circle around the female. Sometimes the courting male carries a blade of grass or feather in his beak. The female signals the male through rapid vertical movements of her tail that she is ready for copulation. This is another characteristic behavior of grass finches that departs from that of true finches, in which the female indicates her readiness by trembling with her wings.

The partners then start looking jointly for a suitable nesting site and begin building their nest. Usually the male

16

gathers the nesting material and carries it to the nest site, where the female then builds the nest. Grass and parrot finches always build a totally enclosed nest with an entrance and exit on one side only. Some species add a more or less elongated entrance tunnel. Size and shape of the nest can vary considerably between species. It is usually ball-shaped or somewhat flattened. In some species the nest is small (8 to 15 cm diameter) and substantially larger in others (20 to 25 cm diameter). The nest-building material consists mostly of grasses; the grasses are used either fresh or dried, depending on the species. Many finches pad their nests with feathers, hairs or other soft materials. Often it is hidden among dense bushes or small trees. Thorny bushes seem to be preferred locations, as are places near wasp nests or even in the lower foundation structure of large birds-of-prey nests, all sites which give protection against predators. Some birds build their nests directly on the ground or in the grass tufts; others prefer hollow trees or deserted parrot or kingfisher nesting sites inside termite mounds.

A peculiarity is the 'sleeping nests' built by some grass finches. These nests are even built outside the normal breeding season, since these birds always spend the night inside a nest. Other species spend the night just sitting on a branch.

The eggs of grass finches are snow white. A clutch consists usually of 4 to 7 eggs, occasionally more. It is difficult to determine the exact length of the incubation period; apparently this varies from 12 to 16 days. The precise time depends upon several factors: temperature, humidity and intensity of incubation. Both partners take turns (about 1½ hours each) sitting on the eggs. Some pairs have been observed to leave a nest unattended, which of course, results in cooling of the eggs and thus delays the development of the embryo. As a rule, intensive incubation commences when the third egg has been laid. Therefore, the first 3 young often hatch at the same time; the remainder

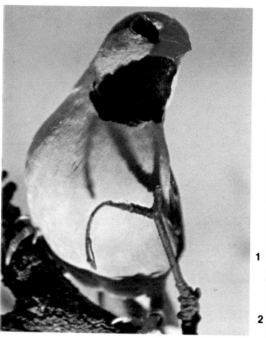

Long-tailed grass finches (1 and 4) are very common and fairly reliable during breeding activities, yet pretty choosy before mating. 2. Female zebra finch. 3. Red-headed and a black-headed Gouldian finch. 5. A pair of Bengalese finches and one male zebra finch.

4

5

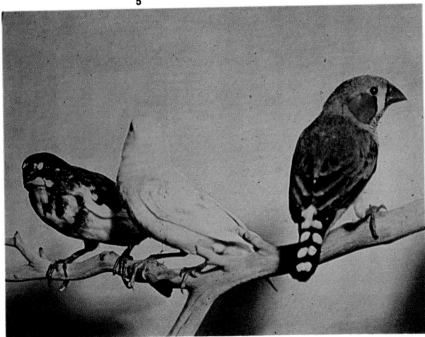

hatch two to three days later, since the last eggs were laid after incubation had already commenced.

Newly hatched grass finch young have a yellowish brown beak that turns black within a few days. After the young have left the nest and within 2 months or so the beak will get its species-specific coloration. Parrot finches have a yellow beak as juveniles—often with a dark cross band over the upper mandible. Young grass finches nearly always exhibit conspicuous mouth and throat markings of dot and line patterns. While these are species-specific, there are, however, considerable resemblances among closely related species. In addition, many exhibit a spot pattern on their tongue and lower mandible, some species have light-reflecting yellow, blue or white papillae with a black margin, consisting of connective tissue. Presumedly the markings indicate the location of the young nestling in the semi-darkness of the nest, thus aiding the parents in feeding their young. The mouth and throat markings and the light papillae disappear with age.

The young are cared for and fed by both parents. During the first 9 to 12 days after hatching they are attended to during the day by both parents. At night the parents usually sleep inside the nest.

The adults will regurgitate part of their crop contents into the beaks of the nestlings to feed them. This food consists usually of half-ripe or sprouting seeds, with some small insects added. During the feeding procedure the young adopt a characteristic begging position; facing one parent, they will press their heads down against the nest floor and open their beaks wide. In most grass finch species the young will press their wings against their bodies while being fed. Some species will raise either one or both wings steeply.

The young birds of most species will usually leave their nest after 21 days. Rice finches, banded finches and red-headed parrot finches can take a few days longer. The young will be called back to the nest by their parents for feeding and to spend the night there. After a few days the adults will also feed them outside the nest, and soon thereafter they will begin picking up seeds from the ground on their own. As a rule, the adults will continue to feed their young outside the nest for about 14 days, and within 2 to 3 weeks after they have left the nest they will feed on their own. After 8 to 10 weeks the young will undergo their first molt, which lasts about a month and ends with the young birds getting their full adult plumage. In some species the young will never return to their nest after they have left it, although they will spend the night close by.

The eggs of grass finches are snow white. A clutch consists usually of 4 to 7 eggs, occasionally more. It is difficult to determine the exact length of the incubation period; apparently this varies from 12 to 16 days.

The black-ringed finch or Bicheno finch, *Stizoptera bichenovi*, (1, 3, 5), is very choosy when looking for a mating partner. The masked grass finch, *Poephila personata* (2), needs all kinds of live food during the breeding season. The diamond finch, *Zonaeginhus guttatus* (4), is known for its bad habit of eating too much and becoming very lazy in captivity.

4

5

There is one golden rule in bird keeping which must be adhered to all times; newly acquired birds must always be changed over *gradually* to different conditions and different foods.

Getting Started

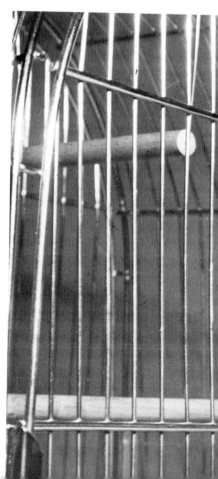

The first thing a new finch enthusiast should do is to find a suitable location in the home for a bird cage. Only after this has been determined should the budding bird hobbyist go out and actually buy the cage and set it up according to the directions provided in this book. Feed and sand should also be purchased when the cage is purchased so that all necessary ingredients are on hand.

Grass finches have always been popular as cage birds, particularly for the beginner who lacks experience, since there are a number of suitable species available to him. Of course there are also those that are rather difficult to keep. Only experienced bird hobbyists should attempt to keep

1

2

3

he painted finch, *Emblema
picta* (1, female; 4, male) is
ery difficult to acclimatize
and even after this period
s recommendable only for
experienced aviculturists.
The diamond finch (2, 3) is
difficult to breed, as its
season falls within the
vinter in many parts of the
US. The beautiful firetail,
Zonaeginthus bellus (5),
has always been rare in
captivity. The bird is very
sensitive to dampness and
easily falls prey to enteritis
and respiratory problems.

4

5

the more difficult species; they provide the opportunity to make interesting and useful observations, but they demand specialized care.

Beginners should start out with easy-to-keep species. Sufficient knowledge and experience can be gained without having to spend too much time on them. This also determines whether the newly gained enthusiasm for birds is really a sustaining, lasting interest. Only then should the beginning bird fancier increase his collection of birds, and so any bird hobbyist who has served such an 'apprenticeship' of one to two years, will then be able to handle the more difficult species later on.

There is a difference between acclimated and newly imported birds. Birds that have been in captivity for some time and have already adjusted to commercially available seeds and to local conditions are considered as being acclimated. This category includes, of course, birds that have been bred in captivity. Ideally, the beginner should try to obtain only acclimated birds. Although they are almost always more expensive than newly imported birds, they are easier to keep. Pet shops often have acclimated birds available, many times birds purchased from local breeders. Birds bred in captivity are especially recommended for beginners because all relevant information in regard to age, feed and maintenance are available from the dealer. Such birds can be recognized by their neat and clean plumage; newly imported birds often present a rather scruffy appearance.

Since Australia prohibits the export, on a commercial basis, of live birds, most of the Australian cage birds (including those referred to in this book) are now bred in Europe and North America, and the Japanese are breeding Gouldian finches as well as red-headed parrot finches and many other Australian birds on a commercial scale by using Bengalese or society finches as 'foster parents.' Japanese birds are heavily inbred, which of course has substantially weakened the breeding birds as well as their offspring. Therefore, one has to be cautious.

Other grass finches are imported in large numbers from Africa and Southeast Asia; however, these do not belong within the framework of this book. Once again it must be pointed out that due to the rapid air transport and good flight connections, most imported birds arrive in a far better condition than in the early days of ship transport. Nevertheless, even today one has to expect certain losses. The bird fancier, therefore, is best advised to buy his birds only from those dealers who keep their birds in clean and spacious cages, where the birds can be active and thus give a good indication of their condition. The best indicators for healthy birds are a full, firm chest, active movements and obvious pleasure in taking baths. Disease symptoms will be discussed in detail under the appropriate chapter later on in this book.

Newly acquired birds, regardless of whether they have been already acclimated or have been recently imported, should be kept separate from other birds in a special quarantine cage. It is only too easy to transmit diseases from newly-arrived birds to established stock. A box cage placed in a warm, draft-free place where it can get sufficient light is ideal as a quarantine facility. Initially, such a cage should be kept in an elevated position, preferably even in a separate room. This makes the newly-arrived birds feel secure and guarantees that they will not be disturbed by other birds. All new arrivals should be kept isolated for a month before they are placed together with other birds.

All newly imported birds should at first be kept fairly warm (at about 25 °C) before they are gradually, over a period of two weeks or so, acclimated to room temperature. Since grass and parrot finches come from largely tropical countries, temperatures should not be allowed to fall below 18 °C. Newspapers should be placed on the bottom tray of the cage; by removing one sheet daily one can monitor the

Star finch, *Bathilda ruficauda,* also known as the rufous-tailed finch. The subspecies *B.r. clarescens (1)* is usually darker in color than other races (2, 3). All star finches are favorites among hobbyists because of their peacefulness and liveliness as well as their readiness to breed.

2

3

digestive process of the birds. Solid droppings indicate proper digestion; yellowish and watery feces are usually signs of some gastro-intestinal problem.

Newly imported birds usually have not been getting sand (grit) and minerals. If both of these are suddenly offered in unlimited quantities, the birds have a tendency to overfeed, which then often leads to digestive difficulties. Instead, they have to be started out on these items in small quantities so that their digestive system becomes adjusted gradually. Sand and minerals are given in shallow containers (saucer, etc.), initially placed in the cage for a period of only about half an hour and then slowly increased. After a few weeks, sand and minerals can then be offered in unlimited quantities. Acclimated birds that have no digestion problems can be given sand and minerals immediately. If gastro-intestinal problems appear to be present, however, the sand and minerals must not be offered. Instead, pulverized charcoal should be given.

Drinking and bathing water should always be accessible to grass and parrot finches. Newly imported birds should be offered only pre-boiled water during the first few weeks; the water can be gradually mixed with unboiled dechlorinated water in subsequent weeks. Tap water should always be left standing in a covered container for several hours before it is given to the birds.

At the time of purchase, the dealer should be asked as to what food the birds have been feeding on (whether it was vegetable food, sprouting seeds, insects or mixed diets) and how the birds can be changed over to other types of food and feeding methods. There is one golden rule in animal keeping which must be adhered to at all times; newly acquired animals must always be changed over *gradually* to different conditions and different foods.

Many finch keepers have come into the finch fancy as a result of their keeping of canaries. Regardless of the specialty area eventually adopted, beginners should always start out with easy-to-keep inexpensive species.

A cage can never be too large. Box cages should have a light-colored coat of paint on the inside and be placed alongside a wall opposite a window. Outdoor aviaries (below) must have a bright, draft-free and dry enclosed section, which can also be heated.

Cages
and
Aviaries

Grass and parrot finches can be kept in cages as well as in indoor or outdoor aviaries. The accommodation for these birds depends largely on the available space and facilities. Many species are, however, not quite suitable for cages. Such birds must be given indoor aviaries at the very least, especially when breeding success is hoped for. If these birds are kept in cages, consideration has to be given to their high level of activity by giving them sufficiently large, roomy cages. Some species, however, can easily be kept in cages, provided certain basic rules are followed.

CAGES

There are two basic cage types, open cages and box cages. Open cages consist of a wooden or wire frame surrounded on four sides and on the top with galvanized wire mesh. The frame sits on a sturdy base that has a removable metal drawer as a bottom. For ease of maintenance cages in excess of 1 meter in length should be equipped with two smaller drawers instead of one large one. Unfortunately, in some commercially available cages the base and drawer are too low. The roof of the cage can be either flat or slightly arched. The ratio of length to width (depth) and to height should be about 4:2:3 (e.g. 80 cm x 40 cm x 60 cm). Such a ratio is particularly important for small cages. Again, for ease of maintenance it is better to have several doors instead of just one; all sections of the cage can then be reached without difficulty. Most suitable are vertically sliding doors, which can be purchased already made. A rather convenient arrangement consists of two doors in the front of the cage on each lower corner. This enables the hobbyist to place feed dishes inside the cage without unduly disturbing the birds. It is also essential to have one larger door, through which branches and nests or nestboxes can be introduced. All-metal cages are rather expensive and often they are not available in the required size or shape. Usually such cages are hexagonal or octagonal and have built-in a number of toys such as ladders, bells, towers and other items that increase the price and provide a lot of hiding places for bird parasites. Such cages are totally useless. Hobbyists are also warned against purchasing brass cages: bathing or drinking water, splashed against the brass, will cause oxidation, which then can lead to poisoning of the birds. Suitable cages can be home-made of galvanized weld-mesh wire with a mesh size of $1'' \times \frac{1}{2}''$ and a wire thickness of 1.24 mm (18 gauge). The base and removable drawers can be make in any welding workshop. Wooden cages are popular with some fanciers, but they are hard to disinfect and keep clean.

Box cages usually consist of a converted wooden box or crate in which a wire front has been inserted in one of the large sides. Lightweight metal (aluminum) or plastic boxes can also be used for this purpose. Box cages must also have a removable drawer; the slot through which the drawer is removed must have a hinged lid. If it doesn't, birds can escape through the open gap. Wire fronts of different sizes are commercially available or can be made to measure.

Box cages should have a light-colored coat of paint on the inside and be placed alongside a wall opposite a window. This permits as much light into the cage as if it were a conventional wire cage. Light from one side only leaves a box cage too dark, so such cages should be kept only in a very bright room.

Box cages have a number of uses; to acclimate newly arrived birds, as breeding cages and as flight cages. Their size depends upon the intended use and on the species to be accommodated. Anyone who builds his own wooden frame or box cages can adjust the sizes to fit specific purposes. Several cages of the *same type* not only look good, but also facilitate easier feeding and maintenance, even if they are *not the same size*. One always has to remember A CAGE CAN NEVER BE TOO LARGE. The following are some recommended cage dimensions for different purposes and various species.

As a breeding cage for a pair of zebra finches or society finches or as a general cage for some of the smallest estrildine finches, the dimensions 60 cm long x 30 cm back to front x 40 cm high can be used. For the easily bred black-throated finch, *Poephila cincta,* long-tailed finch, *P. acuticauda,* or the masked finch, *P. personata,* about 100 cm x 50 cm x 80 cm is quite adequate. Difficult species require larger cages of about 120 to 200 cm length, with corresponding width and height dimensions. In such long cages, a nest is placed at either end, partially covered by dense branches, and feed dishes are placed in the middle of the cage. The birds are obviously more at ease when adequate hiding places are provided.

INDOOR AVIARIES

Indoor aviaries are basically only large flight cages taken indoors. Usually they are made of wooden frames covered with wire mesh. Depending upon their size, they have two or more trays at the bottom as well as several hatches, through which food and drinking containers are placed into the cage. Doors must also be provided higher up along the sides so that branches and nests can be placed inside. Ideally, an indoor aviary should be placed on a stand, about 30 to 40 cm above floor level. The ratio of dimensions should be similar to those given for regular cages. Various suitable indoor aviaries are commercially available, as well as individual components for home assembly of such aviaries. It is best to place an aviary along a wall, because birds feel less at ease in one standing in the middle of a room. It should also be close to a window so that during the summer months the birds can get direct sunlight through an open window.

THE BIRD ROOM

The bird room is a room used solely for birds. It must be bright, dry and heatable, and its windows should face south, southeast or east. Ideally such a room should be subdivided into aviaries made of weld-mesh wire; the aviaries should be situated about 50 cm to 60 cm above floor level. Such an arrangement permits the birds to be easily observed and controlled, and aggressive species and specimens can be isolated. In front of the aviaries must be a passageway, used when feeding and watering the birds, as well as to accommodate some smaller cages for various purposes. These aviaries should be constructed in such a way as to provide about one cubic meter per breeding pair. The windows in any bird room will have to be covered with wire so as to prevent any accidental release of escaped birds.

OUTDOOR AVIARIES
Outdoor aviaries for the purpose of keeping grass finches MUST have a bright, draft-free and dry enclosed section, which can also be heated. One half of the aviary must be roofed over, and the enclosed section should have electrical lighting. At night the birds are always locked up in the enclosed section.

A suitably selected accommodation is of paramount importance in successful aviculture. Unfortunately, it is not possible to discuss cages, indoor and outdoor aviaries in greater detail within the restricted framework of this book. Therefore, I would like to draw the reader's attention to the book *Building an Aviary* by Carl Naether and Dr. Matthew M. Vriends, (published by T.F.H. Publications, Inc., Neptune, N.J.) in which various points are discussed in greater detail. Also, *All About Finches* by Ian Harman and Dr. Matthew Vriends (T.F.H.) is a necessity for every bird fancier.

All weaver finches build completely enclosed nests low to the ground or even on the ground. This fact has to be taken into consideration when aviaries are being built for these birds. Many weaver finches will readily accept artificial nest supports upon which they then build their nests. Several different models of such artificial 'nests' are commercially available. Very popular as an artificial nesting aid is the typical canary shipping cage. This is a small wooden cage originally used for exporting canaries from Germany. Unfortunately, these miniature cages are rather fragile, and nowadays they are rarely available. All that needs to be done to them is to remove a few of the bars along the narrow sides; the birds can then select an entrance and exit. A piece of foam rubber with some nesting material on top is placed at the bottom of the little cage, and the birds do the rest. I have constructed nests out of welded wire mesh with ½″ mesh, something that can be made in any required size. The front end is left half open, and a piece of foam rubber of suitable size (12 x 12 x 12 cm to 15 x 15 x 15 cm or larger) is fastened to the bottom of the nest. Roofed-over basket nests are also commercially available, but they are nearly always too small, with an entrance opening which is commonly not large enough. Larger basket nests having wooden lids can be easily cleaned and maintained.

Long nest boxes, commonly used for parakeets, are also eagerly accepted by grass finches. Such boxes, which are invariably too small for parakeets, are rather ideal for finches. One should always fasten a piece of foam rubber to the inside bottom. In the event a breeding pair has been a bit careless in their nest construction, the eggs will not end up on the bare wooden floor or over the bottom grate of the box. One should always select relatively large nest containers, since birds will always utilize the excess space.

Nests are always placed at various levels in the aviary, but never exceeding a height that cannot be reached without a ladder. They should also be sufficiently camouflaged with twigs and branches attached to the aviary wire. Individual nests should be spaced apart, with branches creating visual barriers. The branches should be positioned one above the other, but staggered horizontally so that droppings from birds above do not fall on the ones below. The branches must not impede the flight patterns of the birds. It is therefore advisable to use several small branches instead of a few large ones. Natural sticks (pencil thickness), instead of machine-made dowel sticks, should be used as perches in an aviary. They must be attached to the side walls of the cage so that the birds are not hindered when turning in flight. Most useful are two perches halfway up the sides, and below these—but offset in the manner of the branches—two more. Some thin climbing twigs are also required for the smallest of the grass finches.

During the winter months the flight space has to be illuminated for at least 12 hours daily. Fluorescent lights have been particularly useful for this purpose. During the night a dim nightlight should be left on, because in total darkness the birds tend to panic, which can have disastrous consequences.

In a combination flight and shelter, you have a strongly constructed and very practical aviary, the size of which may be enlarged to suit your special needs and location. It can readily be used for finches, parakeets or other birds. Painted a suitable color to harmonize with its immediate surroundings, this birdhouse will be an ornament in any garden.

Apart from millet, plain canary seed is also very important in the diet of grass finches. Individual grains must be yellow, shiny and dust free. Several small-grained varieties (below) are preferred by grass finches.

Feeding and Care

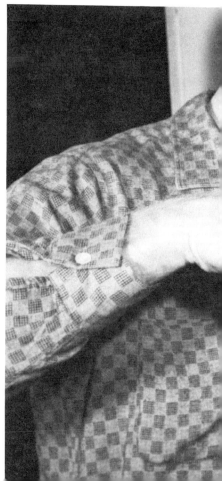

In the wild, grass and parrot finches feed predominantly on ripe and half-ripe seeds, as well as on insects. Some birds will become totally insectivorous after having fed their young on insects. Seed remains the staple diet for most species in captivity, but they also require some animal proteins.

SEEDS

The diet staples in this category are the various millet seeds and plain canary seeds. Supplementary seeds will be discussed later on. The large-grained, thin-shelled white

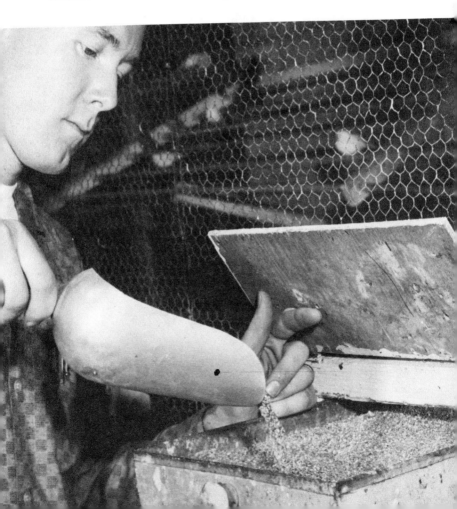

millet is preferred by the larger birds, but it is less popular with the smaller species. Yellow millet, although of comparable size, has a considerably thicker shell and is therefore less suitable for grass finches. Small estrildine finches as well as the larger ones are also very fond of the three small-grained millets: Senegal millet, which is yellowish, round or oval shaped; the closely related Mohar or Indian millet, with its yellow or brown grains; and the smallest, Algerian millet, which has grains of reddish yellow coloration. Most grass finches are very fond of ears of millet, which are usually Senegal millet. These entire seed pods of millet are imported from France and Italy, and lately even from China. They are particularly nutritionally good for newly imported birds or young birds that have just left the nest. Unlike as in the old days, these millet ears are not placed in the cage or aviary in bundles; they are suspended individually so that each ear is accessible from all sides. It is best to offer germinating seeds, since this kind of food is invariably preferred by the birds. Japanese millet as bird seed is relatively new; it came to Europe and North America only after World War II. This millet differs from those described above because its gray-brown seeds are irregularly shaped and have distinct edges and corners. This millet sprouts very readily and is a highly nutritious food.

Apart from millet, plain canary seed is also very important in the diet of grass finches. Individual grains must be yellow, shiny and dust-free. Several small-grained varieties are preferred by grass finches. The best canary seed comes from Morocco and western Turkey.

Although millet and canary seed are the main dietary items, other seeds can be offered intermittently for variety. I usually give a mixture of niger, blue poppy seeds, grass and lettuce seeds twice or three times a week, either scattered over the bottom of the aviary or given in a separate dish (about a teaspoonful for each pair of birds). Shelled oats are also eagerly taken by many of the larger grass finches, and in my opinion this kind of food is an absolute must for acclimating parrot finches. Also eagerly taken by many of the larger birds are germinating wheat grains. Unshelled rice is a good supplementary food for Java sparrows, mannikins and some parrot finches, but most other species will not take to it.

Only the highest quality seeds are acceptable as bird food. Cheap and contaminated seeds can endanger an entire bird stock. Each type of seed is purchased separately so that the aviculturist can prepare his own mixture. Only this assures us that our birds get the required, highest quality diet, tailored to the specific demands of each species. It is impossible to recommend a seed mixture that would be universally satisfactory for all birds. Large species have to get more white millet and canary seed, as well as the small-grained millet varieties; small species feed predominantly on small-grained millets. Ultimately, the best feeding results will be determined by the proper ratio between the various seeds. I prefer a standard mixture that I can adjust by adding supplementary seeds: 4 parts each canary seed and white millet mixed with one part each Senegal, Mohar, Algerian and Japanese millet. Of course, each type of seed can also be offered in a separate dish; even in large cages, however, there would not be enough room for all feed dishes, so a carefully prepared mixture of seeds has to be offered. In large aviaries each type of food can be offered separately, yet even then things can get quite difficult and cumbersome when several aviaries have to be attended to regularly. To top off several dozens seed dishes each day requires a considerable amount of time.

GERMINATING SEEDS

Apart from dried seed grains we must also offer germinating seeds to our birds. During the winter months especially these sprouting seeds replace, to some extent, green food and half-ripe seeds. Getting seeds to germinate is just a matter of practice; it can be learned easily. For grass finches we use the various millets as well as canary seed. Millet can be left to germinate in a mixture, but canary seed—because it requires about 24 hours longer than millet to geminate—should be kept separate. Oats and wheat grains should also be kept separate.

Germination of seeds can be accomplished in several different ways. In one popular method, water is run through a seed mixture in a strainer. Then the strainer with its content of seed is placed in a container with water. The water is replaced after several hours and the seeds are rinsed thoroughly once more, then returned in the strainer to the water bath and left there overnight. Next morning the seeds are rinsed thoroughly once more and then left in the strainer for several hours so that all excess water can be run off; the strainer should be shaken repeatedly. After that the seeds are placed in a glazed earthenware container, covered with a sheet of glass and put in a warm place. After 24 to 36 hours tiny sprouts will appear, and the seeds can then be fed to the birds. It is important that the sprouts are not permitted to grow too large, because the birds will not feed on them as eagerly then.

A similar method is used to get the stalks of spray millet to germinate. They are kept in water that is frequently changed for about 24 hours. After that they are bunched up, placed inside plastic bags and suspended upside-down. Inside the tightly sealed bags a very high humidity will develop; depending upon the temperature, the humidity will cause germination within 24 to 36 hours.

GREEN FOOD

Half-ripe seeds tend to complement the birds' diet rather nicely, and they are particularly valuable while young birds are being raised. Of the green foods, chickweed (*Stellaria media*) must be named first and foremost. Other plants eagerly eaten by many birds are dandelion (*Taraxacum vulgare)* shepherd's purse *(Capsella bursapastoris)*, knot grasses *(Polygonum)*, groundsel *(Senecio vulgaris)* and clover *(Trifolium pratense)*. It is, of course, very important that these plants be collected only in areas that have not been sprayed with insecticides. Before the plants are given to the birds, they are placed into a bucket of water for at least an hour. Then the green food is washed and placed in a strainer so that excess water can run off. Leaves that are not immediately fed should be spread out over a wire frame to prevent decay. Lettuce and spinach have the advantage of being nearly always available, but even they have to be checked for the presence of insecticide (a point which ALWAYS has to be remembered when dealing with green food).

Hobbyists with only a few birds can improvise a supply of green food by sowing canary seed or millet in shallow earth-filled wooden boxes. As soon as the plants have grown several centimeters, the entire box is placed inside the cage or aviary.

FRUIT

Although grass finches normally do not feed on fruit, in captivity they will adjust to it quite readily. A nail is placed through one of the perches and a piece of fruit is skewered onto it so that the birds can easily see it. Sooner or later they will start picking on it, and eventually they will get a taste for it. I have tried several kinds of fruit and have found that the birds will prefer sweet oranges, which supply natural, healthful vitamins. To give the estrildine birds, with their usually rather delicate beaks, adequate access to the flesh of an orange, it is advisable to pierce the cut surface repeatedly with a knife.

OTHER USEFUL FOODS

Grass finches in the wild will feed their young mostly on insects, although the young will also accept half-ripe seeds.

Providing live insects (these birds also like spiders) in captivity is not always easy. Some insects can be bred, but not all of them are suitable for raising young birds. If spiders and insects (flies, grasshoppers and green aphids—black aphids are not eaten by grass finches) can be provided regularly and in sufficient quantities, raising the young of even the most difficult species is no great problem. However, in reality it is almost impossible to find insects in sufficient quantities, since their abundance is very much dependent upon the season. Therefore, it is important to remember that even when insects are periodically available in quantities they should be given to the birds only in moderation so that the birds will still take some of their regular foods. After all, one usually does not know when the insect supply will run out again. The birds easily adjust to live insects as food, and if the insects are given in excess the birds will not only become selective, but also will stop feeding their young if this choice food is not offered anymore.

There are also, of course, other sources of live food, such as mealworms (the larval form of a beetle, *Tenebrio molitor*), which can easily be bred. However, grass finches will take only very small worms, which are usually available from pet shops. Also commercially sold in some pet shops are mosquito larvae, small crickets, fruit-flies *(Drosophila)*, waterfleas and whiteworms (enchytraeids). A good substitute for insects is young ant pupae and hard-boiled egg yolk. Ants of the genus *Lasius* are common in sunny areas in any garden or yard, and their pupae can easily be picked up with a spoon from under rocks or decaying pieces of wood. They can be stored (refrigerated) for several days in a bucket with soil from an ant nest. These ant pupae are excellent food, particularly for rearing small estrildine finches. Pupae of the large red forest ant *Formica rufa* are also excellent food for rearing young birds throughout the year.

Dried out pupae are usually not taken by grass finches, even if they have been moistened with hot water, carrot juice or milk or if they are mixed with hard-boiled egg. This then brings us to another important food for rearing young birds: eggs. Egg food is prepared by the following method: an egg should be boiled for 12 minutes. It is then squeezed through a fine sieve (strainer) and mixed with finely ground breadcrumbs until the entire mass is loosely 'lumpy' without being sticky. This mixture is fed as thin layers in shallow containers. If it is too moist it will easily spoil, particularly in warm weather. To be cautious it is best to offer small amounts of this a couple of times daily, possibly in the morning and again in the evening, and, if need be, once in the middle of the day. The birds are very curious and usually will immediately take the food, especially when they observe that it is replaced regularly.

Several brands of rearing food are commercially available, but I am in no position to assess their nutritional value.

VITAMINS

Vitamins are important for the health and reproductive capabilities of birds. Vitamin supplements are particularly important during the winter months, when green food is not available and there is insufficient sunlight. Some commercially formulated products are designed to contain all essential nutritional elements and contain all essential amino acids and natural fruit sugars which are essential for the proper assimilation of amino acids, especially during periods of stress. In addition, I also mix the same vitamin compounds with germinating seeds and with soft foods, such as eggs, which are then offered to the birds three to four times per week. A vitamin D deficiency can inhibit the uptake of calcium, which can cause the birds to become eggbound.

MINERALS

Minerals are important in the diet of birds for the formation and maintenance of their plumage and bones and in the production of eggshells. A variety of calcium and mineral mixtures are commercially available. Calcium and minerals are scattered over the sand on the aviary floor. The sand should be pure beach sand, which contains, in addition to the very fine sand grains, also some larger grains (shell particles) that are picked up by the birds and aid in their digestion (so-called shell grit). One has to be cautious and watch for oil-polluted beach sand.

WATER

Drinking water for cage birds is best provided in automatic dispensers ('drinkomats') made of plastic. These gadgets can be easily fastened between the wire bars. They should be cleaned and the water renewed every second day. Grass and parrot finches like to take a bath, and bathing water should be provided in a shallow dish placed inside the cage. Alternatively, one of those glass or plastic bird bath houses can be suspended from one of the cage doors. Personally, I prefer a shallow bath container inside the cage. Drinking water in aviaries is best provided in automatic bird water dispensers; plastic dispensers are preferable. Bathing water is poured into shallow containers that are placed inside larger dishes; this prevents the sand from becoming wet from splashing water.

FEEDINGS

The daily seed ration should be given to the birds in shallow containers with a relatively large surface area. Deep containers with a small surface area are unsuitable, since the birds tend to perch on the rim while feeding and the empty seed shells drop back into the bowl, where they soon can cover the entire surface so that the birds cannot reach the uneaten seeds anymore. I use dishes with an opening of

50

about 15 cm, 13 cm, and 10 cm wide; the respective lips are 5 cm, 4 cm and 3 cm high. These dimensions merely indicate the preferred shape of seed dishes; the actual sizes used depend, of course, on the species and number of specimens that have to be fed. In a cage, seed dishes are placed so that bird droppings cannot contaminate the seed and in a manner which will not unduly disturb the birds.

Soft foods (germinating seeds, egg mixtures, etc.) should also be offered in the same kind of dishes, since the birds are already accustomed to them. Depending upon the species and number of specimens which have to be fed, the seed dishes are emptied daily or every other day; the husks are then blown away, and the seeds are placed in a strainer to remove any dust. Afterwards the seeds are returned to the dish. In this manner we can determine the birds' seed preference, which has to be taken into consideration when the dishes are filled again. Dishes for soft food have to be cleaned or replaced with new ones for each feeding. Soft food should be replaced every morning; if young birds are being raised, food dishes have to be changed two or three times daily to prevent spoilage of the food. Such frequent dish changes have the advantage that the curious adult birds will invariably go to the newly replaced food dishes and start feeding, which in turn encourages their young to do the same.

Birds not accustomed to egg mixture or germinating seeds will often ignore such food and pick out only the dry seeds. This seems to be more common in cage birds than in those kept in aviaries. Should it happen, one can sprinkle some soft food over the seeds and thus gradually coax the birds onto soft foods.

Aviary birds are fed in a similar manner. The different seeds are placed in separate dishes inside larger plastic or zinc dishes, which prevents seeds and husks from spreading all over the aviary floor. For some years I have been using relatively large plastic boxes (50 cm x 35 cm x 10 cm) for most seeds, except niger, poppy, grass and lettuce seeds, which are given in separate containers. For grass finches I mix the various millets with canary seed and sprinkle the mixture as a thin layer inside the boxes so that the birds can selectively pick out their preferred seeds. Even when the boxes are used the seeds have to be cleared of empty husks and cleaned of dust once or twice a week. At the same time when the boxes are filled up again we can observe which type of seed is being preferred by the birds. This method is an excellent time-saver, especially when several aviaries have to be looked after. Here, too, care has to be taken that the boxes are not placed directly under the perches, thereby preventing contamination from bird droppings. In the event a box has become excessively dirty it can easily be cleaned.

For soft food I also use plastic boxes (35 cm x 25 cm x 6 cm). I cover the bottom with a thin layer of fine dry sand, upon which the germinating seeds, egg mixture and other soft foods are placed. Every morning the left over food and the sand are discarded and replaced with new sand and food. When young birds are being raised, this procedure has to be repeated around mid-day and in the evening as well. Additional feedings during the day can be made merely by adding food to the boxes, since dried-out food usually does not spoil. In my opinion the birds prefer to pick their food off the sand—which is more in line with their natural behavior—than to take it out of a dish.

Finally, a few words about the now widely used automatic feeders. They come in different models and usually have separate compartments for different seeds. Such feeders consist of an upper storage container for the seeds, which drop down into the actual feeding dish, and a lower container for the empty husks. All models work on the principle that they reduce the feeding workload, and indeed they have to be replenished with seed only once a week. Care has to be taken that the seed channel from the storage container does not become blocked with dust and sand. A disadvantage of automatic feeders is that it can be critical when some birds, especially new arrivals or young ones, cannot find their food supply and consequently starve to death; therefore, I do not recommend the use of automatic feeders.

CARE AND MAINTENANCE

Fresh air, light—ideally sunlight—and the required temperatures are the prerequisites for the well-being of grass finches. Cages and aviaries must always be bright and draft-free. When adjusting the temperature, one always has to remember that wild grass and parrot finches are tropical birds that are rarely exposed to prolonged cold periods. They do best at temperatures of about 20° to 22°C. Slightly elevated temperatures are advantageous during the breeding season. Efforts to acclimate these birds during cold winter temperatures are pointless and thus little more than outright cruelty.

Newly imported birds should be kept at about 25° until they have become adjusted; then the temperature can be *slowly* lowered. As a rule *all* changes, including dietary adjustments, should be made gradually. Grass finches kept in aviaries adjacent to houses should be let outside only on sunny, warm days, and only for short periods. Personally, I prefer not to let my birds venture outside during the winter months. If, however, they are kept indoors in cages, they should be transferred to outdoor aviaries only at the onset of summer, and then only if the aviaries have a well-insulated enclosed section. In any event, I recommend that the birds always be locked up at night.

Grass finches have to be watched that their beaks and particularly their claws do not grow too long. Should this happen they have to be trimmed back, and while doing this the clearly visible blood vessel in each claw must not be damaged. For this procedure the bird is kept in one hand;

you should hold one foot at a time against the light and then cut each claw *below* the blood vessel.

Cleanliness of aviaries and cages is very important and must always be maintained without going to extremes, because the birds should not be disturbed unnecessarily. In a cage, the sand on the bottom is —depending on the number of birds kept—replaced once a week, if need be more often. Breeding cages containing one pair should be cleaned only once a week. In aviaries, the sand directly below the perches and branches is replaced every week, but the entire layer of bottom sand is renewed only every two months, provided there are no breeding birds or those raising young. Branches and twigs are exchanged once every six months or as needed. Nests and nest boxes are removed after the young have left, but care has to be taken that the adult birds have not begun to breed again. Should a nest be occupied again it must not be disturbed. Those nests and nest boxes which have been used should be washed out with hot water containing a disinfectant agent. Grass finches are as prone as canaries to mite infestations. At a major annual cleaning all birds are caught and taken out, and the bottom sand, the nest and branches are removed. After that all sides, the bottom and the wire are thoroughly washed with hot water.

When catching the birds, one has to be careful; it is best to trap the birds in a large metal cage placed over a food dish, with the two sliding doors held open by a thin but strong string. It is importatnt that a cage with *two doors* be used for this purpose, since an aggressive bird sometimes prevents the others from getting to the feed dish. As soon as a bird has entered the cage the doors are dropped, and the bird is thus trapped. It is advantageous to use some 'delicacies' as bait, because birds will learn quickly that there is something special inside this cage and can thus be trapped more easily and quickly. Of course, catching birds in this manner requires some patience, especially when

54

there are some cautious birds in the aviary. However, the great advantage of this method is that it does not upset the birds too much. When there are breeding pairs or those raising young in the aviary one should not attempt to catch any birds.

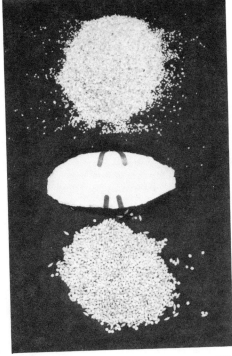

Next to seeds, minerals are very important in the diet of birds for the formation and maintenance of their plumage and bones and in the production of eggshells. A variety of calcium and mineral mixtures are commercially available.

Feeding the ever-hungry babies and continual breeding will severely weaken the adults, particularly the female. Therefore, after two or at the most three clutches the parent birds (below) should be removed and given a rest for some months in a cage without nesting facilities.

Breeding

Many of the grass and parrot finches are easily bred in captivity if they are given the proper care and attention and as long as the required nesting facilities are available. Any initial breeding success is very much dependent upon the choice of species. Not all of them will reproduce easily and willingly in captivity, but three species—the zebra finch, Bengalese society finch and white Java sparrow—are consistently bred in such numbers that they can almost be considered as being domesticated. Some species will breed only under the most favorable conditions, while a few will not breed at all in captivity. Generally speaking, however, most species breed rather willingly as long as at least some

marginally good conditions prevail. Soon after introduction into an aviary the birds begin to build nests; then they deposit their eggs and start to incubate them. Still, it has to be remembered that it is a long road from the first egg to the time when the young birds leave their nest. The most persistent disappointments are encountered by experienced as well as beginner hobbyists during the time the young birds are being raised. Sometimes without any apparent reason the adults stop feeding their young or simply throw them out of the nest. The reason may be that the parents have an inadequate diet or the parent birds are too young and 'inexperienced' as breeders, or perhaps they were disturbed, which often happens when breeding takes place in a cage instead of an aviary.

Therefore, there are two major prerequisites if breeding is to succeed. The first prerequisite is that only healthy birds in good condition and not too young be used for breeding. They must be at least nine to ten months old. Since the age of newly acquired birds is rarely known, one should wait about six months before any breeding is attempted. Generally speaking, grass finches will breed for three to four years, occasionally one or two years longer. They reach a maximum life span of about seven or eight years. The second prerequisite is that the breeder have a true pair—male and female—on hand. Sometimes it is difficult even for an experienced aviculturist to correctly sex a pair, especially when both partners have no conspicuous differences in their plumage. In such a case one should retain an option for a subsequent exchange with whoever supplied the birds. To be on the safe side it is advisable to acquire three or four pairs. The individual birds are marked with a colored leg band; by observing their behavior together true pairs can be determined. Incidentally, this method is also recommended for birds with clearly distinguishable sexual differences, because naturally mated pairs are invariably better breeders than those which have been arbitrarily placed together. The males can usually be recognized by their singing, but sometimes it takes quite a while before the birds start to vocalize.

Newly imported grass finches retain their natural breeding cycle corresponding with the seasons of their country of origin, but in subsequent years they will adjust their breeding activities to local seasons. When a suitable bird room with proper illumination and heating is available, breeding can be done without regard to the season. Minimum temperatures should be 19 °C, even when the birds are not breeding.

In captivity grass finches sometimes breed repeatedly in quick succession. As soon as one lot of youngsters have left the nest, the female may immediatley lay eggs again. Sometimes the female begins to incubate a new clutch while the young birds from the previous clutch are still in the nest. This process will continue and even accelerate if the parent birds are not stopped. Continual breeding will severely weaken the adults, particularly the female. Therefore, after two or at the most three clutches the parent birds should be removed and given a rest for some months in a cage without nesting facilities. Sometimes a female may continue laying eggs even there, but there is very little that can be done about it. Here it should be remembered that it is not the laying of eggs which is exhausting for the female, but rather the incubation and feeding of the young that place an energy drain on her. Grass finches do not keep their nests clean, so after each clutch the nest should be removed and thoroughly cleaned before being returned to the aviary.

The best breeding facilities are sparsely populated bird rooms or aviaries. Here one has to remember that each breeding pair requires about one cubic meter of space. If this minimum space is provided even the young birds, after they have left their nests, can remain in the aviary, which is beneficial for their growth and development. Moreover, birds will mate far more readily in a spacious aviary than in a small cage, and females are less prone to become egg-bound.

If, however we are forced to use breeding cages, the instructions given in the section on cages should be followed and the recommended cage dimensions complied with. My experiences have shown that it is best to have only one breeding pair per cage. Personally, I would only keep grass finches together in one aviary, but some of the smaller true finches, such as waxbills and some of the African or South American finches, can also be placed in the same aviary. However, since true finches are rather territorial and aggressive, only one pair each should be kept in the same aviary. Diamond doves, which are among the smallest doves, also can be kept together with grass finches in the same aviary. Normally doves do not disturb other birds, but sometimes it takes a while before the other birds have become accustomed to the doves. The same can be said about adding some of the grass parakeets (Bourke's, turquoise, scarlet-chested, etc.) to grass finch aviaries. Much depends on the temperament of individual birds. It is important that birds be closely watched.

It is also imperative that suitable nests be provided. Several different models are commercially available. It is advisable to have two or three nests for each pair so that fighting is avoided as much as possible. These nests are attached to the aviary walls at different levels and as far apart as possible, but they should always be accessible for inspection without a ladder. These nests come equipped with small hooks that permit easy attachment and removal. If there also are some branches affixed to the aviary walls, the birds have an opportunity to build their own nests. Availability of proper nest-building material is even more important, so a variety of materials should be offered to the birds. These materials can be hay, straw, fresh grass during the summer months, moss, coconut fibers (about 15 cm long), feathers, etc. Threads and thread-like material (agaves) should not be used, because the birds could conceivably cut their feet. Although it is best to have several nests for each pair of birds in an aviary, for a breeding cage usually one or two nests are adequate. In a cage, the nests are attached close to the ceiling in the far corners. Species that will breed in a cage are easily bred in any event and do not appear to be very choosy. Breeding attempts with more difficult species should be made only in larger cages of about 150 to 200 cm in length, which permits food and water to be given in the middle of the cage without disturbing the birds nesting at the end. Very practical is a cage with two drawer bottoms, which can be divided into two smaller cages by inserting a piece of glass or a wire partition in the middle. This way the birds can be confined to one side while the other side is being cleaned.

Each clutch consists of four to seven eggs, rarely more. In the event a clutch is very large there is a possibility that it is from two females. All grass and parrot finch eggs are pure white. Incubation usually begins when the third egg has been laid. It lasts 12 to 16 days, and both parents will sit on the eggs alternately. When breeding birds are off their nest while feeding it is best not to check out the nest; it would only upset the birds. In any event, a bird sitting on eggs should NEVER be removed from the nest.

Provided the eggs have been fertilized, quite often up to three young may hatch simultaneously; the others will follow at intervals of a day or so. During the hatching time one has to be very patient so that eggs believed to be infertile are not prematurely removed when indeed they may only require some additional incubation time. Hatching can be delayed because the onset of incubation may have been delayed or the parents may have been absent from the nest for some time. Both of these factors are very difficult to assess.

Once the young have hatched, they will remain in the

nest for 21 to 23 days; they will not leave all at the same time. Nests should never be inspected until *after* the young have left for good. Any such action may cause the young birds to leave the nest prematurely, which can be disastrous. Even if they were placed back inside the nest they will have been sufficiently disturbed so that they would only leave again and then probably die.

Once the young, at least those of some species, have left the nest under normal conditions they can still be rather helpless for a few days. They could fall behind the nest, become wedged between branches or drown in the water dish. In aviaries the latter can be avoided by placing a flat rock in the bathing container or removing the container completely and replacing with an automatic water dispenser. A week after the young have left the nest they are already quite adept in getting around the aviary. They should be left there until they have their adult plumage. In sufficiently large aviaries they are usually not bothered by their parents. It is important to band the youngsters with colored leg bands so as to distinguish them from successive generations.

When a cage is used for breeding it is often better to remove the adults as soon as the young have become independent; the youngsters should be kept in the cage for some time. When several cages of the same make and model are used and where perches, nest boxes and feed dishes are interchangeable, a transfer of birds is far simpler and easier. In most grass finch species the young become completely independent about 14 days after they have left the nest, but it is advisable to keep youngsters and parents together in an aviary for several weeks. The different types of rearing foods should be continued even after the youngsters have become completely independent from their parents.

Under controlled breeding conditions it is of paramount importance to be able to distinguish individual birds from each other. It is important that the correct ring size be used;

a tight ring could injure the foot, and a ring too loose could slip off or—what is far worse—could slip over the foot joint, pressing the toes together and thus crippling the foot. Some organizations use closed rings, which are slipped over the foot and onto the leg when the bird is still very young. Bird bands (rings) should have engraved on them consecutive numbers, the year and the identification sign of the breeder.

All notable observations and relevant data about the birds should be meticulously recorded for future reference.

Once the young have hatched, they will remain in the nest for 21 to 23 days.

A young zebra finch begging for food; if the birds are properly fed, diseases will be rare. Apart from heat and special diets, sick birds also require specific medication; properly cured for, however, the birds should stay healthy, like the young Gouldians below.

Diseases

Birds in captivity are susceptible to a variety of diseases. The diseases are not always easy to cure, but they can often be avoided through proper precautions. This presupposes, of course, that our birds are constantly watched and immediately isolated at the slightest sign of abnormal behavior. Normally adult birds sleep on one leg only, and young birds just out of the nest sleep on both legs. When we notice an adult bird sleeping on both legs we *must* assume this is a sign of discomfort and thus possibly a disease symptom. Other obvious signs are: fluffed-up feathers, dim eyes, slow movements and loss of appetite. The loss of appetite symptom can be tricky. Sick birds are

often at the feed dish picking among the food, but without really eating anything. The droppings are liquid-like, whitish or greenish. If one or more of these symptoms are noted on a bird, it must be immediately isolated. Transfer it to a quiet, warm cage and give it a special diet. In any event, for tropical birds *heat* is often a very effective treatment, so sick birds should be transferred to a heated hospital cage. Very suitable for this purpose is a box cage with a wire front; the cage should be about 100 cm long, 30 cm deep and 40 cm high with two bottom drawers. These dimensions are adequate for small birds. The bottom is covered with newspaper so that the droppings and digestion can be monitored daily. If digestive difficulties are noted, the birds should not be given sand or minerals; pulverized charcoal should be offered instead.

Half-way up the sides of the cage should be several perches. An infra-red lamp (75 to 150 watt) should be placed in front of the cage, giving full exposure of the radiation to at least the closest perch. Care must be taken that the front wire of the cage does not get too hot, since excessive heat can harm the birds. At first the correct distance for the heat lamp has to be determined (about 10 cm in front of the wire), and once this has been worked out it should be left on day and night. At first the temperature close to the lamp is kept at about 30 °C and at the opposite end of the cage at room temperature (20 to 25 °C). Food and drink dishes are placed on the bottom of the cage so that their contents are not directly exposed to the infra-red lamp. The hospital cage is kept in a quiet room at normal temperature; the sick bird should not be disturbed by the other birds. Quite often the sick bird will stay close to the lamp. As its condition improves it will slowly move farther away into the cage or try to get away from the radiation through other means. Only when it is completely cured should the infra-red lamp be removed. The recuperated bird should be kept in isolation for another week before it is returned to the other birds.

Hospital cages also can be used as quarantine cages for newly arrived birds, particularly imported birds that have not yet become acclimated to local conditions.

It is often rather difficult for the beginning aviculturist to arrive at a correct diagnosis, because a number of diseases have fairly similar symptoms. For small birds we therefore have to select a universal treatment. Most commonly encountered bird diseases have to do with colds or gastro-intestinal problems. Specific symptoms have already been discussed above. A cold can often lead to gastro-enteritis; the bird's abdomen becomes reddened, and the digestive tract becomes distended to the point that it can be clearly seen through the skin. The disease also causes the chest musculature to regress so that the breastbone can be felt.

Birds kept under treatment in a hospital cage are given the same seeds as in their cage or aviary, but in addition some easily digested food should be offered. Good foods in this regard are: germinating seeds, boiled and finely chopped mealworms (boiled for about two to three minutes), possibly also some recently molted 'white' mealworms, spiders, green leaf aphids and other small insects. Especially important—virtually indispensable—are animal proteins for those birds that normally feed on insects. This includes many of the estrildine finches. I have observed frequently that birds placed in unfamiliar surroundings will not accept germinating seeds but will feed without fuss on germinating stalks of spray millet. Pulverized charcoal is another MUST for sick birds in a hospital cage.

Apart from heat and special diets, sick birds also require specific medication. It makes it easier for the bird when it takes medicine willingly and on its own account. This eliminates having to catch the birds and force-feed the medicine, thus avoiding stress which would further exhaust the already weakened bird. Therefore, it is advisable to use mostly water-soluble medications. Fortunately this includes most of those antibiotics that are especially suitable against bird diseases. These are usually available in powder form. On the third day the antibiotic is replaced with thin oatmeal porridge, followed by another two days of antibiotic treatment. If the disease has not subsided after three or four treatments, further efforts are pointless.

Another common complaint is *egg binding*. Sometimes a female is unable to expel a fully formed egg, which means the bird has become egg-bound. There are a number of causes of this condition: the egg is too large or does not have a shell as a result of nutritional deficiencies, particularly lack of vitamins and calcium. Cold and lack of adequate exercise (cage too small) can also cause egg binding. This disease is far more common in cages than in aviaries. Such afflicted females mope around with fluffed-up feathers, sitting in front of the nest or the bottom of the cage or aviary. If the proper treatment is not initiated immediately the bird will die. It should be placed into the hospital cage, which should be heated to 30 to 35 °C. With a small pipette or eye dropper a few drops of slightly warmed olive oil are put into the cloaca. The oil can also be massaged into the abdomen of the bird. Usually the egg is dropped within an hour and the female resumes its normal activities. If the egg is thin-shelled it has to be crushed through gentle pressure from both sides. Since this is a somewhat dangerous operation it should **be done only in an emergency and only by an experienced aviculturist.** A female that has suffered from egg binding has to be carefully watched in the event the condition repeats itself. One of the best things one can do is to give vitamin- and mineral-fortified foods during the breeding season. Furthermore, a female used for breeding should not be too young and should be permitted only two or at most three successive broods.

There are many other bird diseases, but unfortunately they can't be discussed within the limited size of this book. Instead, I would like to recommend the following two books: *Diseases of Birds,* by L. Arnall and I.F. Keymer, and *All About Finches,* by Ian Harman and Dr. Matthew M. Vriends. Both books were published by T.F.H. Publications, Inc., Neptune, N.J. Beyond that I would like to impress upon all beginning aviculturists that they must seek proper veterinary advice when they have a sick bird.

Egg binding may be prevented by adequate diet, enough minerals and sufficient exercise.

Australian grass finches are among the best of breeding finches, and there are several domestically bred strains of common birds like the zebra finch now in existence. It is important for the future of these birds in the avicultural fancy that full attention be given to producing fully domesticated strains of the rarer species (such as the long-tailed finch, below) as well.

Finch Species

Now I would like to describe and discuss briefly the Australian grass and parrot finch species, with the exception of two species—the red-eared firetail finch, *Zonaeginthus oculatus,* and the closely related beautiful firetail finch, *Z. bella.* Both of these species have only rarely been imported into Europe and North America, and then they have never lived for very long. More frequently they have been kept and bred successfully by Australian aviculturists. Nevertheless it is unlikely that these two species will ever reach us in substantial numbers.

Only one parrot finch is regularly imported in large num-

bers, the other species are rarely, if ever, imported. I will discuss only those that are most commonly imported. The scientific names used here are based on *Vogel in Kafig und Volieren; Prachtfinken Band I und II*. Any generic deviations from *Checklist of Birds of the World* have been indicated in parentheses after the corresponding scientific name.

ZEBRA FINCH, *Taeniopygia guttata castanotis* Gould

(Poephila guttata castanotis)

Adult male: General color above, including wings, pale brownish-gray, turning to silvery-gray on head and hind-neck; rump white, sides black; upper tail-coverts black with broad bars of white, extended ones tipped white; tail feathers brownish-black; narrow black line at base of lower mandible followed by white bar with black margin; sides of face and ear-coverts yellowish-chestnut; throat and fore-neck gray with black bars; band on lower fore-neck black; abdomen and under tail-coverts white; flanks chestnut with white spots; beak red; legs and feet yellow-orange; eyes red. Length about 10 cm.

Adult female: Differs from male by having sides of face and ear-coverts light gray to white (instead of chestnut); throat, fore-neck, breast, and sides of body gray; abdomen and under tail-coverts white or pale brownish-yellow.

Immature: Similar to female, but without distinct black-and-white markings on head and with under-surface creamy-buff. Beak black.

The zebra finch has a very characteristic call. It resembles that of a child's toy trumpet, but its call can also be rather variable.

Distribution: Widely distributed throughout the Australian mainland, except Cape York Peninsula, southern Queensland, southern and southwestern Australia. A subspecies, *T. guttata guttata*, occurs on the Indonesian islands of Flores, Sumba, Timor and the Lesser Sunda Islands. It is clearly distinguished from the Australian population by being darker-colored with the crown and nape of an intense brown; the region of chin and throat (malar region) lacks the cross bars. Specimens from this race have rarely ever been imported alive into Europe and North America. The ecology of zebra finches, as well as their behavior in captivity, has been extensively studied by Immelmann and Vriends. They feed predominantly on various grass seeds—which are picked up off the ground—as well as on insects, particularly termites and flies caught in flight. Insects are used mainly for feeding the young.

The nests are constructed in low-lying bushes and hollow trees, and also in protected sections under roof eaves. Often there are several nests close together. Both parent birds build the nest jointly out of dried grasses; the inside is cushioned with softer grasses, feathers and hairs. The female lays four to six eggs, which are incubated alternately by both parents. The fledglings leave the nest after 21 to 22 days.

Zebra finches are very hardy and are therefore the most commonly seen grass finches as cage birds. Most mated pairs are excellent breeders, although failures may occur with some. The best breeding success can be accomplished in thinly populated aviaries. I always keep only one pair per aviary, because sometimes some birds become aggressive and have to be removed. This species will breed even in a cage as long as the dimensions do not go below 60 cm in length.

Over the years several color mutations of the zebra finch have been selectively bred, such as white, silvery-gray, cream-colored, penguin-colored and other color forms.

BLACK-THROATED FINCH, *Poephila cincta cincta,* Gould

Male and Female: Crown and nape gray; hind-neck and upper portion of back cinnamon-brown; lower back and wings brown; rump crossed with black bar; upper tail-coverts white; tail-feathers black; forehead, ear-coverts and cheeks whitish-gray; lores and throat black; remainder of under-surface cinnamon, large black patch on lower flanks; abdomen and under tail-coverts white; beak black; legs and feet flesh-colored; eyes brown. Total length about 10 cm.

There are two subspecies (some authors recognize three subspecies); *P.c. atropygialis* differs from the nominate subspecies in its rich fawn color on back and breast, lighter gray color of the head, and in having upper tail-coverts black instead of white.

The literature indicates a variety of sexual color differences among black-throated finches, especially the throat spot, which is often larger and wider in males than in females, but this is not an unequivocal characteristic. The only definitive difference between the sexes is the typical call of male birds.

The colors of immature birds are less intense; they especially have less red.

Distribution: *P.c. cincta* occurs from northern New South Wales northward to Inkerman and Townsville, and again appears farther north between Cairns and Normanton. *P.c. atropygialis* occurs in northern Queensland, north of Townsville, but only rarely into the northern part of Cape York Peninsula. The southern region forms a transition zone in which several races live together.

The black-throated finch breeds well in a roomy cage and in an aviary, but *P.c. cincta* is sometimes rather aggressive towards other birds, so pairs from this race should be kept alone. *P.c. atropygialis* is always very peaceful.

Black-throated finches build their nests fairly high in half-open boxes, and rarely among branches or in bushes. The inside of the nest is usually lined with soft hay, feathers and hairs. A clutch consists of five to six eggs, and the incubation period lasts 12 to 13 days.

The nestlings will leave their nest after 21 to 22 days, but their parents will continue to feed them for quite some time afterwards. Therefore the young should remain in the aviary for at least another month, because they are very prone to stress problems at an early age. Fresh ant pupae, egg food and germinating seeds (preferably canary seed) are the best types of food for raising the young.

LONG-TAILED FINCH *Poephila acuticauda acuticauda* Gould

The long-tailed finch is very similar to the black-throated finch, although its body appears less compressed and more slender.

Adult male: Crown and nape gray; mantle pinkish-fawn; back and wings brown; upper tail-coverts white; band across rump and tail feathers black; lores black; chin, throat and upper chest black; remainder of under-surface pinkish fawn; large patch of black feathers on each flank; center of lower abdomen and under tail-coverts white; beak yellow; legs and feet bright red; eyes brown. In wild forms the median tail feathers are hair-like and far longer than in those specimens bred in captivity. Total length about 17 cm.

Adult female: Very similar in plumage to the male.

Another subspecies is *P.a. hecki,* which is distinguished by its variable red beak (coral-red to orange-red).

In this species, too, sexing is very difficult, and the only certain way to recognize the male is by its call. Immature birds have a black beak and duller coloration.

Distribution: Northern Australia, from Derby eastward through the northern part of western Australia, the Northern Territory and the Gulf of Carpentaria to the Leichhardt River in the Western part of northern Australia. The yellow-beaked race in the north of Western Australia changes gradually into the red-beaked race, going eastward. The red beak changes in intensity from orange-red to deep coral-red, color variations which also occur in captivity since both forms freely interbreed. The offspring exhibit a number of red variations of the beak. In order to maintain these races or subspecies relatively pure, only birds with similarly colored beaks should be mated so that pure lines of each race can be built up and maintained. Such selective breeding should be done jointly by several aviculturists, with each maintaining meticulous breeding records.

The long-tailed finch breeds well in aviaries, but less frequently in cages. Although most birds are peaceful towards other inhabitants, it is advisable to keep only one pair per aviary. Breeding this species is a bit complicated at times, since only mated pairs will breed successfully. It is therefore recommended that a number of birds be kept together initially until truly mated pairs can be selected; the mated pairs can then be transferrred to individual aviaries for breeding.

This species prefers an elevated nest; all other details are similar to the ones already described for the black-throated finch. Both species are similar in their behavior and requirements and tend to become quite tame in captivity.

MASKED FINCH *Poephila personata personata* Gould

General color above, including wings, light cinnamon-brown, slightly grayer on primaries and lower back; rump and upper tail-coverts white; tail-feathers black; forehead, lores, anterior portion of cheeks, and large triangular-shaped spot on chin and upper throat black; sides of head and under-surface of body pinkish-brown; large black patch on lower flanks; center of abdomen, thighs and under tail-coverts white. The eyes are red, and the beak is yellow and stouter than in any of the other grass finches; feet are coral-red. Total length about 12 cm.

Another geographic race is the white-eared grass finch, *P.p. leucotis* Gould, in which the sides of the head are white, the white extending around the top of the breast adjacent to the black throat. A patch of white also occurs on the lower flanks, immediately anterior to the black area. The beak is light yellow. Immature birds are grayish-brown, lighter under the throat and on the abdomen, with a black beak.

Once again, the call of the male is the only sure distinguishing characteristic between the sexes. Similar to that of the zebra finch and the double-bar finch, the call of this species resembles the sound of a toy trumpet. However, contrary to the other two grass finches, this species is very shy, and it can take a long time before the male begins to vocalize.

Distribuion: Northern Australia, from Derby eastward across the Northern Territory to Cape York Peninsula. The white-eared grass finch occurs in northwestern Queensland in the western and northern region of Cape York Peninsula only.

In the wild the masked finch breeds in bushes and in small trees, possibly even on the ground. In captivity some pairs will nest on the ground, while others prefer highly elevated nesting facilities. As nesting material these birds will use grasses, soft hay, and coconut fibers. The relatively large nest is usually lined with soft plant fibers, feathers and hairs. In aviaries it is advisable to provide canary boxes, half-open nest boxes, larger enclosed nesting baskets and nests made from weldmesh wire.

Masked finches are among the most peaceful of all grass finches, and thus they rarely antagonize other inhabitants in the aviary; a prerequisite is, of course, that the enclosure does not hold too many birds and that they are not aggressive towards each other. The previously mentioned two grass finch species should not be kept with masked finches. Required feeding and care is the same as discussed for the other two species.

DOUBLE-BAR FINCH, *Stizoptera bichenovii bichenovii* Vigors & Horsfield (*Poephila bichenovii bichenovii*)

Adult male: General color above, including crown of head, pale brown, with fine barrings of dark brown, coarser towards the rump; band across rump black, remainder of rump and upper tail-coverts white; upper wings like back, remainder of wings brownish-black, white spotted; tail feathers black or brownish-black; lores, feathers above eye, cheeks, ear-coverts, chin and throat white, bordered with narrow black line, which widens on forehead into a wide band; fore-neck and chest white, slightly tinged in center, and washed with brown on sides of chest, followed by second broad black cross-band; remainder of under-surface white-washed faint creamy-buff; under tail-coverts black; beak bluish-gray; legs and feet gray; eyes dark brown. Total length about 10 cm.

Another race, the black-ringed finch, *Stizoptera bichenovi annulosa,* is distinguished by a black instead of a white rump. In both races the male and female are colored very similarly. Literature references to sexual color differences have rarely been substantiated. Once again, the only sure sign is the call of the male, which resembles that of the zebra finch. The plumage of the immature birds is less bright, and markings appear washed out.

Distribution: Double-bar finch from Cape York Peninsula southward through Queensland into New South Wales; black-ringed finch throughout Northern Territory and northwestern Australia.

The double-bar finch will readily breed in sparsely populated aviaries and occasionally also in large cages. The nest is situated up high, usually in half-open boxes, canary boxes or wire nests, sometimes even in bushes if such are made available to the birds. They use as nesting material mostly dried grasses, coconut fibers and plant twigs. Some birds line their nest with feathers or hairs, others with soft, fine grass. In the wild only the double-bar finch will line its nest; the black-ringed finch does not. A clutch consists of four to five eggs, which hatch after a twelve-day incubation.

The young will leave the nest after three weeks and continue to be fed by their parents for another three weeks. Food for the young should be germinating or half-ripe seeds and egg mixture; the latter will not always be eaten by all birds. I have obtained my best breeding results with this species by feeding a sufficient amount of ant pupae to the young. Despite the export ban in Australia, both subspecies are still available. Apparently many birds are bred each year to provide a sufficient supply. In order to prevent inbreeding, aviculturists should exchange young birds as future breeding stock.

DIAMOND FIRETAIL FINCH, *Zonaeginthus guttatus* Shaw *(Emblema guttata)*

General color above, including wings, brown; rump and upper tail-coverts bright crimson; tail-feathers black; forehead, crown of head and hind-neck ashy-gray; lores black; throat white; broad band on foreneck; sides of foreneck and flanks black, each feather having a sub-terminal white spot; breast, abdomen and under tail-coverts white, sometimes interspersed with a few reddish feathers; beak red; eyes brown with rosy ring; feet dark brownish-gray. Total length about 12 cm.

Males and females have very similar plumage. The literature has many references to distinct differences between the sexes; the most commonly quoted one is that the female is supposed to be smaller than the male and has a chest band narrower than that of the male. Presumably most of these are individual variations, which are unreliable as sexual characteristics. My experience has shown that the beak of the male tends to be darker, almost blackish-red, while that of the female is of a lighter red. These features seem to apply only to adult birds, and they are not infallible. The only reliable difference between males and females in many grass finches is the call of the males. The advertising call of the male has a higher pitch and is more drawn out than that of the female.

Immature birds: Back and wings olive brown; rump and upper tail-coverts crimson; tail-feathers brownish-black; head grayish-olive; cheeks and ear-coverts olive-gray; sides of foreneck and flanks olive-brown with wide bars of grayish-white and a few blackish-brown feathers with white subterminal spots; remainder of under-surface white.

Distribution: Eastern Australia from southern Queensland southward through eastern New South Wales and southeastern Australia to the Eyre Peninsula and Kangaroo Island.

Diamond firetail finches were imported fairly early, particularly between the two world wars and after World War II, until the export ban in 1960. Nowadays, only birds bred in captivity are available; since this species breeds very readily, its stock is substantial.

It takes various millet seeds and canary seed, also germinating seeds, especially stalks of spray millet. Various greenfoods should be offered regularly, as well as animal proteins such as egg mixture, mealworms and small insects, especially fresh ant pupae. The latter are particularly important when raising young.

Since diamond firetail finches have a tendency to get fat they should not be kept in cages, but instead in sparsely populated aviaries. During the breeding season many mated pairs are somewhat aggressive, and other birds are driven off from the vicinity of their nests. Sometimes individual males persistently chase other birds to a point where already weakened birds can easily be killed. Such difficult pairs must, of course, be kept in a separate aviary.

Breeding is complicated only by the fact that most diamond firetail finches are rather choosy about their partners. Once again we should enable the birds to find their own partner by observing a group of color-banded birds in an aviary. Frequent observations will soon indicate which

80

birds have paired off, and they are then removed into a separate aviary for breeding purposes. Such selectivity assures substantially increased breeding successes.

Diamond firetail finches build rather large nests, often in bushes and among branches, something that has to be taken into consideration when an aviary is set up. However, many pairs will also accept canary boxes, half-open nest boxes or welded wire nests. The nesting material consists of long grasses, straws, shepherd's purse plants, leaves, coconut fibers and sisal hemp. The nest is usually lined with hay, feathers and hairs. These birds are very active nest builders, so building material should always be available. A clutch consists of five to six eggs, and the young leave the nest 24 to 25 days after hatching. However, they do require another three to four weeks until they are completely independent. Then they should be removed; if not, the parents will attack them. More than three successive broods should not be permitted before the pair is given a prolonged rest.

PAINTED FINCH, *Emblema picta* Gould

Adult male: General color above pale brown; rump and upper tail coverts scarlet; tail-feathers dusky brown; lores, forehead, fore-part of cheeks, chin and upper throat scarlet; fore-neck, breast and abdomen black, spotted white; irregular line of scarlet down center of breast; under tail-coverts black; beak: upper mandible black, tipped red, lower mandible red with blue base; legs and feet flesh-colored; eyes whitish. The beak is conspicuously long and pointed. Total length 10.5 cm.

Adult female: Differs from adult male in having only lores, feathers above eye and at base of lower mandible scarlet; under-surface duller black, with white spots larger and with less scarlet on center of breast.

Immature birds: Similar to female, but substantially duller; head and breast without red; white spots on under-surface smutty; beak: upper mandible black, lower one gray with whitish base.

Distribution: Dry desert areas in the interior of Australia and the northwestern regions, from the coast of Western Australia to northwestern Queensland.

The painted finch has only rarely been imported. Importation increased somewhat after World War II up to 1960. Nowadays, only locally bred birds are available, or some that are occasionally imported from Japan. Aviculturists keeping painted finches should take great care to avoid excessive inbreeding and thus maintain good blood lines of the existing stock. This species is totally unsuited for cages; instead it should be kept in sparsely populated aviaries. In the wild it lives in rocky hill country with spinifex grass. In accordance with its habitat the painted finch is a typical ground dweller (Immelmann), a fact that has to be taken into consideration when the aviary is set up. It must contain a densely planted bush area as well as sufficiently open ground. The bottom should be covered with sand and topsoil and some flat rocks. Since painted finches will spend the night neither in their nest nor on branches, but only on smooth surfaces, some boards should be provided in the aviary along one wall, about 50 to 100 cm above ground. Only a breeding female will remain at night in her nest. In the wild the painted finch prefers a solid base for its nest: lumps of soil, small stones, charcoal, pieces of bark, dry grasses or small twigs. Therefore, the aviary has to contain similar materials. The birds build their nest about 50 cm above ground, where they prefer a free-standing nest, or they may chose hollow logs, larger half-open nest boxes or even canary boxes. Apart from the usual nesting material such as hay, grasses, coconut fibers and the like, painted finches also require some branches with a rough surface, such as dried evergreen branches. However, the individual branches must not be longer than 15 cm. As an inner cushion for the nest the birds use soft materials such as hairs, feathers and plant fibers.

The clutch consists of four to six eggs. The incubation period varies with the season; during the summer it lasts about 15 days and during the winter about 19 days (Immelmann). Often parents will abandon their brood and start laying eggs and incubating again.

Painted finches prefer the smaller millet varieties, but animal foods such as ant pupae, small mealworms, spiders and leaf aphids are important for the well-being of these birds. Green food and germinating seeds, particularly stalks of spray millet, also are necessary. For rearing young birds it is vital to provide a wide selection of animal food and green food.

RED-BROWED FINCH, *Aegintha temporalis* Lath.

General color above, including the upper wing-coverts and inner secondaries, dull olive yellow, brighter at sides of hind-neck; primaries dusky-brown, margined olive; rump and upper tail-coverts crimson; tail-feathers dusky-brown; crown of head and nape leaden-gray; superciliary stripe extending onto sides of nape crimson; ear-coverts, throat and under-surface ashy-gray, washed pale buffy-brown; beak red, with triangular-shaped black patch on culmen and on center of lower mandible; legs and feet flesh-color; eyes reddish-brown. Total length 12 cm. No sexual differences in plumage. Males can be recognized with certainty only by their call.

Immature birds: General color above dusky olive-green, under-surface grayish brown; rump and upper tail-coverts dull crimson.

Three distinguishable though similar races exist.

Distribution: Eastern Australia, from Cape York southward through New South Wales to Victoria and Kangaroo Island. Has also become established in Western Australia in the vicinity of Perth since 1960 or 1961. Also allegedly established in Tahiti and on Viti Levu (Fiji Islands).

Since red-browed finches are fairly delicate and also unreliable breeders, they have nearly disappeared again from the European and North American market since the export ban in Australia. They are best kept in indoor aviaries. Food and care same as indicated for the other Australian grass finches.

PLUM-HEADED FINCH, *Aidemosyne modesta* Gould

Adult male: General color above deep olive-brown, with feathers of rump and upper tail-coverts subterminally barred white; wing-coverts and innermost secondaries deep olive brown, tipped and marked white; primaries brown with paler outer margins; tail-feathers black, the outer ones with a white spot at tip; forehead and top of head dark claret-red to violet ('plum colored'); lores black; ear-coverts white, barred brown; cheeks white with only slight indications of brown cross-bars or tips; chin dark claret red, nearly black; remainder of under-surface white, transversely barred pale olive-brown; center of breast, abdomen and under tail-coverts white; beak black; legs and feet fleshy colored, eyes brownish black. Total length about 11 cm.

Adult female: Similar in plumage to male, with less claret-red on forehead; white tips of feathers on sides of forehead from a line extending from base of upper mandible over eye; chin and throat whitish, without any dark claret spot; white under-surface less conspicuously barred with pale olive-brown than in male.

Immature birds: General color above grayish-brown; under-surface grayish-white with faintly indicated cross-bars.

Distribution: From northern Queensland southward through the interior of eastern Australia to southern New South Wales. Initially the plum-headed finch was annually imported, but in small numbers only. After the export ban of these birds from Australia the importation of plum-headed finches stopped altogether. Therefore, it is now only occasionally available as specimens bred in captivity. The European and North American stock of this species is fairly low, so it is not very often commercially available.

Plum-headed finches are not as active as the other Australian grass finches. They are not particularly suited for cages, and they do not like low temperatures, which should not drop below 18 °C, or even better, not below 20 to 22 °C.

As food we can offer various millet seeds and canary seed, as well as germinating and half-ripe seeds; stalks of germinating spray millet are particularly suitable. Chickweed, as well as young meadow grass *(Poa annua)*, especially with half-ripe seeds, is most suitable as greenfood for these birds. In addition, they have to have animal food such as fresh or deep-frozen ant pupae, small mealworms and other insects, as far as these are available. Egg mixture is not taken by all birds. For raising young, insects and germinating seeds are especially recommended. Many pairs even manage to raise their young on germinating and half-ripe seeds alone.

Under favorable conditions this species will breed very well. Since cages are unsuitable for plum-headed finches, we have to use sparsely populated aviaries with plenty of bushes or shrubs. Aquatic reeds, long and strong grasses or corn plants should also be available for the birds to prevent their claws from becoming too long.

If possible this species likes to build free-standing nests in bushes or shrubs. The nesting material consists of green or dried grasses, straw and coconut fibers, and the inner lining of feathers or hairs. The entrance to the nest is kept narrow. In my aviaries this species has nested in canary boxes, large enclosed basket nests and even in wire nests. Generally the nests are situated fairly low, about a meter above the ground, but I have also seen the birds occupy fairly high nesting facilities.

The clutch consists generally of four eggs, and the incubation period lasts about 12 days. The young leave the nest at the age of three weeks and continue to be fed by their parents for another two or three weeks. Good pairs will breed successively several times and will often start a new brood even before the old youngsters have left the nest. This tends to lead to parental neglect of the young, which then invariably will die. One should not permit more than three successive clutches; after that the parents will need a rest for three to four months in a roomy cage or in an aviary without nests. During the breeding season, plum-headed finches are easily disturbed, and consequently the nests should not be inspected and should be totally left alone.

CRIMSON FINCH, *Neochmia phaeton* Hombr. & Jacq.

Adult male: General color brown; feathers of back washed dull carmine; upper tail-coverts bright crimson; upper wing-coverts and innermost secondaries like back, outer secondaries brown margined on outer web dull crimson; primaries brown, edged yellowish-brown; central pair of tail feathers dull crimson on outer webs; center of forehead and crown of head and neck ashy brown, with purplish-black sheen on feathers of forehead and crown; lores, line of feathers over eyes, sides of face, ear-coverts and under-surface rich crimson-red, with small white spots on some feathers on sides of breast; center of lower breast, abdomen and under tail-coverts black; beak red, base of lower mandible whitish; legs and feet yellow. Total length about 13 cm.

Adult female: Differs from male in having forehead and crown ashy brown like the back; crimson on lores, sides of face and throat much duller, and fore-neck and breast ashy brown spotted white on sides; center of lower breast and abdomen light brown, getting slightly darker on under tail-coverts.

Immature birds: General color above, including sides of head, dull grayish-brown; upper tail-coverts and outer margins of secondaries and tail feathers dull crimson;

throat and upper breast pale brown; lower breast and abdomen fulvous-brown; beak black.

Distribution: Neochmia phaeton phaeton, the nominal race of this species, occurs from the northern region of Western Australia eastward through northern Australia and into northwestern Queensland. The other race *(N.p. albiventer),* which is characterized by white under tail-coverts and a white abdomen, occurs only on Cape York Peninsula. This form has rarely been imported. A very similar race occurs in southern New Guinea. Crimson finches have been imported only rarely, but somewhat more frequently during the last 10 years prior to the Australian export ban. Nowadays only captive-bred specimens are available. This species is very sensitive to low temperatures, and thus it should not be kept below 20 °C. It is the most aggressive of all the grass finches so far discussed. Even in the wild, crimson finches will drive off substantially larger birds, such as doves and parakeets, from the vicinity of their nests. Therefore it can only rarely be kept together with other birds. An indoor aviary of about 2 to 3 cubic meters volume is most suitable for a single pair of crimson finches. Since these birds like to climb among branches and only rarely venture to the ground, the aviary should have adequate branches and tall bunches of reeds.

Crimson finches rarely build free-standing nests, so they should be provided with canary boxes, half-open nest boxes, boards affixed along the walls of the aviary and other nesting opportunities at different levels in the aviary. They require larger nests than most other grass finches, with dimensions of about 15 cm x 15 cm x 20 cm or larger. The nesting material used consists of grasses, straw, coconut fibers, reeds and other fibers. It is also important that large amounts of white feathers and hairs for cushioning the nest be available to the birds.

The clutch consists of five to eight eggs. Incubation starts after the fourth or fifth egg has been laid. During the day both birds will alternate sitting on the eggs; at night only the female will sit. The young develop rapidly, and upon leaving the nest they can already fly quite adequately. They are then not fed as long as other grass finch youngsters are fed by their parents.

Crimson finches will breed successively, but not more than three broods should be permitted in one season. The birds have to be watched closely so that the young can be removed as soon as the parents become aggressive towards them. This species prefers a variable diet, so the birds should be offered not only the ususal seed mixtures but also a native seed mix. Apart from dried seeds they must also have germinating seeds, particularly stalks of millet, which have been brought to germination. Greenfood is important, as is animal food, such as fresh ant pupae. During the breeding season crimson finches are almost exclusively insectivorous, and breeding success is very dependent upon the availability of sufficiently variable animal foods.

As long as the proper conditions are provided crimson finches will breed quite well in captivity. They need their own aviary with a choice of nesting facilities, fairly high temperatures and a variable but specific diet with emphasis on greenfood and insects.

STAR FINCH, *Bathilda ruficauda* Gould
(Neochmia ruficauda)

Adult male: General color above olive-brown, slightly browner on wings; upper tail-coverts dull carmine, each feather tipped with a large white spot suffused pink; central pair of tail-feathers dull carmine, remainder dusky-brown washed dull carmine on outer webs; entire fore-half of head, ear-coverts, chin and upper throat crimson, ear-coverts and upper throat with tiny rounded white spots; lower throat, fore-neck and sides of the body light olive-gray, each feather having white spot near tip; center of breast and abdomen yellowish-white, paler on under tail-coverts; beak red; legs and feet yellowish; eyes red. Total length about 11 cm.

Adult female: Color pattern generally duller than in male, less red on head.

Immature birds: General color above, including wings, dull olive-brown; lores and feathers above and below eyes gray; central pairs of tail-feathers dull carmine, remainder dull olive; under-surface much paler than upper parts; abdomen whitish; beak black; legs and feet brown; eyes yellowish-brown.

We distinguish two races, *Bathilda ruficauda ruficauda* and *B.r. clarescens. B.r. ruficauda* has less extensive red coloration around the head and is grayish-green above, with a pale yellow under-surface. *B.r. clarescens* has a very extensive red coloration around the head and is greenish above with a more yellowish abdomen. In addition, there occur in the wild as well as in captivity a number of transitional forms (hybrids), including some in which the male has so little red on its forehead that it can be mistaken for a female. Many of the intermediate forms are indiscriminately interbred in captivity, and males with bright red head colors are eagerly sought after. This has also produced a very pale, nearly yellow, mutant in captivity, considered to be recessive in relationship to the normal coloration of star finches.

Distribution: *B.r. ruficauda* central Queensland, southward to Rockhampton; *B.r. clarescens,* northern and northwestern Australia and northern Queensland.

In the wild star finches build their nests close to the ground in grass tufts or low shrubs, but also in trees up to 7 m high. Generally they seem to prefer dense bushes where they can build free-standing nests. Therefore, aviaries should be equipped so that nesting facilities are provided at different elevations. My birds have always preferred canary boxes, which always have been placed fairly high. The desired nesting material is fresh and dried grasses, hay, coconut fibers and, for lining the nest, light feathers and hairs.

A clutch consists usually of three to six eggs, which are incubated alternately by both parents during the day and only by the female at night. The incubation period lasts about 12 days, and the young leave the nest after about 21 days. From then on the young are still fed by their parents for another two weeks or so. This species will also breed continuously, but breeding pairs should be removed after three broods and given a rest for several months in a large cage or aviary without nesting facilities.

Provided star finches are kept in a sparsely populated aviary they will breed very willingly; they are peaceful towards the other inhabitants. While they are generally rather hardy, they are susceptible to damp colds. During the winter months the temperature should not drop below 15 °C, and if the birds should be breeding the temperature must not fall below 20 to 22 °C.

The required diet is similar to that of the other grass finches discussed before. It should always include germinating seeds and, when possible, half-ripe seeds and greenfood. These birds also require a certain amount of animal protein in the form of fresh (or frozen) ant pupae and small live insects. If nothing else is available small mealworms can be used; the mealworms, however, should not be considered to be a proper substitute for the ant pupae. Star finches usually will not take egg mixture, but one should try it anyway.

GOULDIAN FINCH, *Chloebia gouldiae* Gould

There are three recognized color forms of this species; they are distinguished from each other by black, red or yellow coloration of the upper part of the head. Originally they were considered to be three distinct species, but they seem to be merely three different color forms of the same species. That is, they are not three geographically restricted races. In the wild all three forms can occur within the same population, and they are found over the entire geographic range of the species. Furthermore, all three forms will mate indiscriminately with each other. The black-headed form appears to be more widely distributed than the red-headed one, while the yellow-headed forms is rarely encountered in the wild. Because of breeding in captivity the yellow-headed form seems to be increasing in numbers, but there appears to be no significant difference in the frequency of occurrence among the three forms when bred in captivity.

Red-Headed Form

Adult male: General color above, including upper wing-coverts and inner secondaries, grass-green; primaries and outer secondaries brown, edged dull grass-green; rump and upper tail-coverts bright cobalt blue; tail feathers black; lores, cheeks and ear-coverts, forehead and occiput dull scarlet, bordered by narrow line of black, widening into black patch on upper throat, and followed by band of bright cobalt-blue, broader occiput; fore-neck and chest lilac, margined below with narrow yellowish-orange band; breast, sides of body and abdomen rich yellow; center of lower abdomen and under tail-coverts white; beak grayish-white, tipped red; legs and feet yellow; eyes dark brown. Total length about 15 cm.

Adult female: Similar in plumage to adult male, but much duller.

Black-Headed Form

Adult male: Similar to red-headed form but without scarlet on head, lores, cheeks, ear-coverts, forehead and occiput, these being entirely black.

Adult female: Similar in plumage to adult male, but much duller.

Yellow-Headed Form

Adult male: Similar to red-headed form, but having regions of yellow instead of dull scarlet.

Adult female: Similar in plumage to adult male, but colors are seldom as distinct as they are in males; also have a fair amount of black pigmentation interspersed, similar to red-headed females. The beak is horn-colored, with a yellow tip.

Immature birds: Head, cheeks, sides of neck and hind-neck ashy gray, shading into greenish-olive of back, wings and tail; primaries blackish-brown, margined on outer webs yellowish-olive and on inner webs buffy white; under-surface ashy brown, paler on chin, center of breast and under tail-coverts; upper mandible blackish with nodules of opalescent coloring around nape, lower mandible reddish-white, tipped red; legs and feet light brown; eyes brown. The first molt starts at an age of six to eight weeks, and it is normally completed in three to four months, which can become extended under unfavorable conditions. Gouldian finches should not be bred until they are a year old.

Distribution: Northern Australia, from approximately Derby in northwestern Australia eastward through northern Australia to the southeastern shores of the Gulf of Carpentaria and into northern Queensland, except Cape York Peninsula. Southward the range of Gouldian finches extends into a latitude of 19°. Thus Gouldian finches occupy the warmest regions of Australia, with temperatures of 40 to 45°C in the shade during the breeding season. This information was provided by Professor Immelmann, who has studied this species in the wild for some time. He observed that Gouldian finches have the greatest need for elevated temperatures of all Australian grass finches. Therefore, during the breeding season temperature must never drop below 22°C, even better 25 to 30°C; during the remainder of the year Gouldian finches should never be exposed to temperatures below 18°C. It is also of paramount importance that an adequate humidity be maintained, which should be about 55% at 20°C and about 70% at temperatures of about 25°C or more. This species is par-

92

ticularly sensitive during its molting period and while eggs are being laid; it is therefore pointless to 'experiment' with low temperatures during these critical periods for the birds.

Whoever wants to work with such interesting but rather difficult species must do an extensive literature review on the subject and seek advice from experienced aviculturists. This way disappointments and set-backs can be avoided.

Gouldian finches should be bred as individual pairs separately in large box cages of about 120 cm to 150 cm length, 50-60 cm width (depth) and 80 cm height. Inside the cage we place different nesting facilities such as canary boxes, half-open nest boxes of similar size or wire nests, at different levels inside the cage. Apart from pencil-thin perches, some branches and twigs among which the birds like to climb about should be attached to the walls of the cage. This species can also be bred in aviaries, jointly with several other pairs, provided at least 1 to 1.5 cubic meters of space is available for each pair.

As food we offer predominantly canary seed and stalks of spray millet as well as other kinds of millet, because it is important that the diet be kept variable. Germinating canary seeds and similarly sprouting stalks of millet must be offered daily. The latter is a particular delicacy for the birds. If possible we should also offer half-ripe seeds of different grasses, chickweed seeds and dandelion seeds, as well as the leaves of chickweed, dandelion and young lettuce. In the wild the young are being raised mostly on insects—flying termites, ants and others. In captivity we replace natural insects with fresh ant pupae, egg food and small mealworms. In order for new birds to become accustomed to such insect 'substitutes' it often helps if they are temporarily kept together with other birds that are already well familiar with this type of food; their feeding encourages the new birds to feed on these unfamiliar foods.

Gouldian finches can be bred successfully in suitable cages if favorable temperatures and humidity are maintained and a variable diet are offered. The females have a tendency to become egg-bound easily, so the diet has to be heavily fortified with vitamins and minerals.

In the wild, Gouldian finches tend to breed in hollow logs, crevices, etc., and thus in captivity they prefer prefabricated nesting facilities. Since they use a variety of nesting materials in nature, they should also be given ample choice in captivity, such as green and dry grasses, straw, coconut fibers and other plant fibers. Long threads should be cut down to 10 or 12 cm. Gouldian finches do not cushion their nest with feathers or hairs.

Generally speaking, a clutch consists of four to five eggs. The incubation period lasts about 14 to 15 days, and the young will normally leave their nest 22 days later. Once they have left they begin to gather food on their own within a few days, however, the parents will continue to feed them for another two weeks. As soon as the youngsters have left the nest, the female will begin to lay eggs again, yet the adults should only be permitted two or at the most three successive broods before they should be given an extensive rest period.

Breeding in captivity, particularly by Australian aviculturists, has produced a number of color mutations such as albinos, lutinos and blue colored specimens. The lutinos have a yellow plumage with a red head mask and red eyes. The blue specimens have sky-blue instead of green back and wing feathers. According to my information nothing so far has been published about the genetics of these mutations, and in fact, such birds have never been imported, presumably because of the Australian export ban.

The genetics of the three different head colors have been fairly well documented and should be mentioned here briefly. The hereditary factor for red-headedness is sex-linked and is dominant to that for black-headedness (Immelmann). Black-headed birds, therefore, are always pure black-heads; red-headed females are always pure red-heads, while red-headed males may either be pure red-heads (have two factors for red-headedness) or split for black-headedness (have one factor for red-headedness and one factor for black-headedness). As both types look exactly alike, the hereditary basis of a red-headed male may be penetrated only by breeding experiments. When pairing Gouldian finches the following breeding results are possible:

1) Black-headed male X black-headed female = black-headed males and females.
2) Red-headed male X red-headed female = red-headed males and females.
3) Red-headed male X black-headed female = red/black-headed males and red-headed females.
4) Red/black-headed male X red-headed female = red-headed males, red/black-headed males, red-headed and black-headed females.
5) Red/black-headed male X black-headed female = red/black-headed males, black-headed males, red-headed females and black-headed females.
6) Black-headed male X red-headed female = red/black-headed males, black-headed females.

The yellow head color is recessive to black as well as to red head color. The theoretical expectations are as follows:

1) Yellow-headedness X yellow-headedness = all offspring are yellow-heads.
2) Yellow-headedness X normal colors = all offspring are normal (split to yellow-headedness).
3) Yellow-headedness X normal (split to yellow-head) = 50% yellow-headed and 50% normal (split to yellow-head).
4) Normal (split to yellow-head) X normal (split to yellow-head) = 25% yellow-head, 25% normal, 50% normal (split to yellow-head).

PICTORELLA FINCH, *Lonchura pectoralis* Gould
Adult male: General color above, including forehead and

crown, grayish-brown; primaries brown, pale on outer webs; upper wing-coverts brown, with minute white dot at tip; tail-feathers dusky-brown; lores black; sides of face, ear-coverts and throat glossy purplish-black; fawn line extends from sides of forehead over eye to sides of neck, where it is much broader and slightly brighter; breast white, feathers having subterminal black bar, concealed except at sides; remainder of under-surface light vinaceous brown; under tail-coverts light brown, with dusky wash on apical portion, which has ill-defined cross-bar and broad tip dull white; beak bluish-gray; legs and feet flesh color; eyes dark brown. Total length about 12 cm.

Adult female: Similar in plumage to male, but feathers on sides of face, ear-coverts and throat are brownish-black. Those on breast have somewhat broader subterminal black bar, giving whole breast a black-and-white barred appearance.

Immature birds: Dark brownish-gray, little lighter on under-parts. Beak brownish-black.

While the median tail feathers in all other *Lonchura* species are elongated and pointed, those in the pictorella finch are rounded off at the end. This is also the only species in which there are distinct color differences between males and females. In other *Lonchura* finches both sexes have more or less identical plumage.

Distribution: Northern Australia, from Derby eastward through the Nothern Territory to eastern Queensland, southward to Charters Towers.

Pictorella finches have only rarely been imported, and since the Australian export ban they have become rarities. Therefore only locally bred specimens are sometimes available. This species can be bred fairly easily, but it still remains relatively rare. As all northern Australian birds are sensitive to low temperatures, the species should never be kept below 18 °C.

As far as the dietary requirements are concerned this

species is not particular. Apart from the usual seeds, these birds should also have germinating seeds, greenfood and animal proteins daily. Even white worms (enchytraeids) have been accepted in one case.

In the wild pictorella finches build their nests close to the ground in tufts of grass or in low bushes and shrubs; in captivity, however, they often choose elevated locations for their nests. Aviaries especially set up for these finches should have tufts of grass and dense branches to be used by the birds as nest supports; some pairs will even prefer canary boxes and other nesting facilities. Nesting material includes grasses, straw, coconut fibers, small twigs and similar items. The nest is usually lined with soft grass. A clutch consists of four to six eggs. Once the young have left the nest they will be completely independent within two weeks. In six to seven months they will have obtained their adult plumage.

CHESTNUT-BREASTED FINCH, *Lonchura castaneothorax* Gould

Crown of head, nape and hind-neck grayish-brown with darker streaks; back and wing-coverts dark cinnamon brown; wing-feathers grayish brown, margined with the color of back; rump and upper tail-coverts straw yellow to brownish yellow; central pair of tail-feathers straw yellow, remainder dark brown with yellow margins; lores, sides of face and throat black; fore-neck and chest pale chestnut; black band across lower chest and bordering sides of breast; remainder of under-surface white, marked on sides of abdomen with cinnamon and black, with black flanks and under tail-coverts; beak bluish-bray; legs and feet leaden-gray; eyes brown. Total length about 12 cm.

Both sexes are identically colored; the males can be recognized by their distinctive call.

Immature birds: Uniform dark olive brown above, including wing-coverts; secondaries and primaries ashy

1

2

3

1. Female crimson finch, *Neochmia phaeton.* 2. Male Jerdon's finch, *Lonchura kelaarti,* from the open woods and tea plantations of Ceylon and parts of India. 3. Zebra finch. 4. Male crimson finch. 5. Gouldian finch, comparatively expensive and cold-sensitive species.

4

5

brown with brownish buff outer margins; tail-feathers ashy brown; cheeks olive brown with white streaks; throat buff white; upper chest brownish buff; remainder of under-surface whitish buff.

Distribution: From Derby in northwestern Australia through Northern Territory into northern Queensland including Cape York Peninsula, southward to Sydney in New South Wales. On the Australian mainland there are two recognized closely similar races of this species, and there are four more in Papua-New Guinea. This species has been introduced to the Society Islands and to New Caledonia as well as to Tahiti (Vriends).

YELLOW-RUMPED FINCH, *Lonchura flaviprymna* Gould

General color above, including wing-coverts, chestnut brown; wings grayish brown, margined chestnut brown; forehead, crown of head, hind-neck dull gray, cheeks and ear-coverts slightly tinged creamy buff; rump and upper tail-coverts golden straw color; central pair of tail-feathers like upper tail-coverts, remainder blackish brown with paler edges; throat whitish; remainder of under-surface creamy buff, washed fawn on breast and whitish on lower abdomen; under tail-coverts black; beak, legs and feet bluish gray; eyes blackish brown. Total length about 12 cm.

Once again, male and female plumages are virtually identical, and only the call of the male is the distinguishing sexual characteristic.

Immature birds: Indistinguishable from immature chestnut-breasted finches.

Distribution: From Derby in northwestern Australia through the Northern Territory and into northwestern Queensland. This species is not quite as eastwardly distributed as the chestnut-breasted finch, yet both species live jointly and in their shared range. Quite commonly their

100

nests are close together in breeding colonies, and indeed they often interbreed. Prof. Immelmann once noted that 10% of all examined nests were occupied by mixed pairs, which were apparently breeding just as successfully as pairs of the same species. Therefore hybrids are very common and indeed are often found among imports.

The ecology of both species, including their nesting habits and general behavior, is virtually identical. Since the yellow-rumped finch lives in rather warm areas, it is very sensitive to low temperatures and should not be kept below 18 °C during the winter months. Its dietary requirements are the same as discussed for the chestnut-breasted finch. Here I would like to emphasize once more that our cage and aviary birds must always be provided with germinating seeds and greenfood, and during the summer months with half-ripe seeds from meadow grass, *Poa annua,* and chickweed. They seem to be particularly fond of stalks of germinating spray millet, and in fact my birds are also fond of oranges, of which I give daily a small piece skewered onto a nail near a perch. Many pairs will raise their young with germinating and half-ripe seeds only, while others also take a substantial amount of animal foods like mealworms, ant pupae and small living insects. My birds also accept egg mixture and germinating wheat grains eagerly.

In the wild, both species build their nests close to the ground among tall grasses or reeds, but in captivity their nests are situated invariably rather high above ground. The aviary should be decorated as for the chestnut-breasted finch, with opportunities for the birds to build their own nests; the aviary should offer various nest boxes at different elevations as well. Some pairs will breed willingly in an aviary but will refuse to breed in a cage. Since male and female are virtually identical it is often difficult to find a pair. In additon, this species is often rather particular about a partner, so one has to let the birds select their own partners by placing several pairs together in the same aviary.

1 through 5: Views of the lovely Gouldian finch. Breeding Gouldians is a subject for specialization in aviculture. As much has been written by experts in favor of colony breeding as in favor of single pairs per breeding aviary. Most agree that flights of at least six feet are advisable for each pair and that if other Gouldians are to be included, the population should never be crowded in any way.

4

5

Then by observing the birds one can remove obviously mated pairs. A clutch consists of four to six eggs. The young will leave their nest about three weeks after hatching and will continue to be fed by their parents for another three weeks. Adult plumage will be obtained after three to six months.

Hybrids of both species can be rather variable in their coloration. Usually the hue of the chestnut-colored parent prevails. The cross-band of the breast is only weakly indicated in some specimens and is missing completely in others, with the entire abdominal area being yellowish. Hybrids are fully fertile.

PINTAILED NONPAREIL, *Erythrura prasina* Sparrm.

Adult male: Bright blue face, throat, and forehead changing to green on the upper parts; lores darkened by black; rump and upper tail-coverts bright red, duller towards the tail; central tail feathers elongated to a point and brighter, traces of black and green subordinate the outer margin; chest bright red, diminishing in intensity towards lower chest area and over the abdomen; sides are duller and mixed with paler shades, becoming dull buff-colored in the lower region; eyes brown; feet brownish horn colored; beak black. Total length about 14 to 15 cm.

Adult female: Forehead, crown of head, sides and throat greenish or blue. Under-surface brownish; upper tail-coverts red; tail shorter than that of male.

Immature birds: General color above greenish gray; throat gray, under surface brownish white.

A common color mutant is the yellow-bellied nonpareil, or parrot finch, in which the red colors have been replaced by yellows. This red or yellow, respectively, is often overlooked in females, because these colored areas occur only on the upper tail-coverts. Therefore it was once assumed that yellow-bellied mutants occurred only in males. The yellow color is genetically recessive against the red one.

Distribution: Burma, Thailand, Malaya, Sumatra, Java and Borneo. This is the only species of this genus that is regularly imported into Europe and North America. Other species are available only infrequently, and some have never been imported. In the early days these birds were transported by ship, which involved journeys of many weeks during which they were fed badly, and thus they invariably arrived in very poor condition. This situation has, of course, been changed now through air transport.

This parrot finch can be acclimated only with considerable difficulty since it has to adapt to a different diet. It requires ample vitamin supplements, especially Vitamin B and D, which can be given in soluble form added to the drinking water. Seeds, particularly canary seed, white millet and shelled oats, should be mixed with rice to which the birds are already accustomed. In addition to dried seeds we also have to offer germinating seeds, especially canary seed, wheat and oat grains and stalks of germinated spray millet. The proportion of rice is then gradually reduced. Even well acclimated birds require a highly variable diet. My birds are very fond of oranges. It is also important that they receive greenfood and, for raising their young, animal proteins in the form of boiled mealworms and fresh ant pupae, which some birds may not take to very readily.

If this species is kept in a cage it may remain very timid and has a tendency to become fat. Therefore after an acclimating period the birds should be transferred to a well planted aviary. All parrot finches like to bathe, which has to be taken into consideration. Moreover, they also require sufficiently high temperatures. Particularly during the initial acclimating period the temperatures should not drop below 25 °C; later on they may be lowered to no less than 18 °C.

This species is difficult to breed, since it molts twice a year and the molting period often does not coincide for male and female. They will build their nest in shrubs and

1
2

3

1. Pictorella finch, *Lonchura pectoralis;* 2 and 3. Spice bird, *L. punctulata;* 4. Blue-faced parrot finch, *Erythrura trichroa;* 5. Chestnut-breasted finch, *L. castaneothorax.* All species are easy to keep, but breeding is almost impossible. All species need insects.

4

5

bushes but may also accept canary boxes or half-open nest boxes. Some birds will build their nest low to the ground, although most seem to prefer high locations just below the roof of the aviary. Nesting material: coconut fibers, grasses, small leaves and other fibers. The nest is lined with soft grass only. Each clutch consists of three to five eggs, and the incubation period lasts for 12 to 14 days. The young will leave the nest after three weeks, and the adults will continue to feed them for another two weeks. Adult plumage is obtained after three months.

BLUE-FACED PARROT FINCH, *Erythrura trichroa* (Kitt)

Adult male: General color above rich grass green; lores, forehead to behind eyes, cheeks and ear-coverts cobalt blue washed with mauve; rump and upper tail-coverts dull carmine; tail feathers olive brown margined dull carmine; under-surface light grass green, tinged golden olive on thighs; beak black; legs and feet pale brown; eyes brown. Total length 12 cm.

Adult female: Similar to male, but has blue forehead and cheeks less extended and much duller.

Immature birds: Uniform dull green, paler on under-surface, without blue coloring on forehead and cheeks; beak not as dark as in adult. Extent and intensity of blue coloration of head as well as the richness of the green varies between different races of this species. In captivity these races are invariably interbred, and specific characteristics often appear mixed between sexes and different races. The most conspicuous characteristic of males is, once again, their call.

Distribution: 10 different races are distributed throughout the Celebes, the Moluccan Islands, New Guinea, northeast Australia (eastern part of Cape York Peninsula), New Britain, New Ireland, Bismarck Archipelago, Micronesia, Solomon Islands, New Hebrides, Banks Islands, and Loyalty Islands. They are rarely imported, but occasionally birds bred in captivity are available.

Generally speaking, these parrot finches will adapt readily to captivity, and dietary requirements are the same as those discussed for *E. prasina*. They are not particularly well suited for a cage, but they do well in an aviary similarly set up as for the pintailed nonpareil. This species will breed well provided a mated pair can be found, which is not always very easy. Like all other parrot finches they must have sufficient heat, and temperatures should never be permitted to fall below 18°C. Some pairs will build free-standing nests, but most prefer nesting facilities to be provided. Nest-building materials are the same as for the previously discussed species. A clutch consists of four to five eggs, sometimes more, which are incubated for 12 to 14 days. After three weeks the young will leave the nest but will continue to be fed by their parents for another two weeks. By then the plumage of the young is highly variable; some may be all green, others may have more or less blue colors, while others may already resemble their parents. Adult plumage is obtained within three months.

RED-HEADED PARROT FINCH, *Erythrura psittacea* Gmelin

General colors are patterns in bright red and bright green. Forehead, crown of head, sides and throat red; hindneck, sides, back, wing-coverts and under-surface grass green; tail coverts and median, elongated and pointed tailfeathers red; eyes brown; beak black; legs and feet brownish. Total length about 12 cm.

The sexes are difficult to distinguish. Although some references indicate that females have duller colors in general, the red-head colors are supposed to brighter but less extensive. Those characteristics are not very reliable, since they may be found in both sexes. Therefore one should rely on the only safe distinguishing characteristic,

1

2

3

1. Beautiful munia, *Lonchura spectabilis*; 2. Striated munia, *L. striata*; 3. White-headed nun or maja finch, *L. maja*; 4. Yellow-rumped finch or straw-rumped finch, *L. flaviprymna*; 5. Black-headed mannikin, *L. m. atricapilla.* All these species can be kept together in a medium-sized aviary. Breeding successes are extremely rare.

4

5

the call of the male, which consists of an extended long trill, to which the female invariably replies with a very short trill.

Immature birds: Head without red colors, or such red is duller and less extended than in adult birds. All other colors are also duller and tend to be grayish green. Lower mandible and base of upper mandible orange.

Distribution: New Caledonia.

The red-headed parrot finch was imported for the first time into England in 1870. Later on this bird was also imported into the mainland of Europe, where it always remained a rarity, because New Caledonia is under French jurisdiction, and France imposed a tight export ban on this bird. Consequently, only a few shipments reached Europe. However, around 1960 several shipments were made to different countries, including Japan, where subsequently many red-headed parrot finches were bred with Bengalese as 'foster parents.' This led to a number of shipments of captive-bred birds to Europe. These imported birds have to be adjusted carefully and then with considerable patience to the variable diet available in Europe. According to Dr. Burkhard, a specialist in parrot finches, birds imported from Japan will breed only after an acclimation period of 2½ years. Wild-caught birds or their direct descendants are quite rare nowadays.

Even after having been acclimated this species is very sensitive to temperatures below 18 °C, and during the breeding season it requires temperatures in excess of 20 °C. Since red-headed parrot finches also have a tendency to become fat, they should be kept in aviaries instead of cages. They are not particular about their diet; they will accept the usual, and some fruit in addition. Oranges were very popular with my birds. During the summer various green-foods should be offered, such half-ripe seeds *(Poa annua)*, oats and germinating wheat grains. More so than other parrot finches, this species needs animal proteins in the form of boiled mealworms, fresh ant pupae and if possible, living insects such as fruit flies, vinegar flies and aphids. Egg mixture is often rejected by this species. Animal food is particularly important when young are being reared.

Provided they are looked after properly, red-headed parrot finches are among the best breeders of all parrot finches, although many mated pairs will produce infertile eggs or abandon their young without any apparent reason; possibly these birds may have been too fat.

Selecting a pair is difficult, since male and female plumages are virtually identical. Males often appear to be more abundant. Nesting materials used are the same as for the blue-faced parrot finch. Some pairs will build free-standing nests if possible; most, however, will accept nesting facilities (canary boxes, etc.) provided for them. Some will nest close to the ground, but most pairs will prefer elevated locations, often immediately under the roof of the aviary. A clutch consists of four to six eggs, which are incubated for 12 to 14 days. The young will leave the nest after three weeks, and they then continue to be fed by their parents for another two weeks. Provided the proper (animal) food is available the parents will look after their brood very attentively. Sometimes a new brood is started when the previous young are only two weeks old. When this happens usually the male will continue to feed the young.

As with some other grass or parrot finches—Gouldian finches, pintailed nonpareils—there are also yellow-headed mutations among this species. They appeared for the first time in Denmark towards the end of the 1940's. These were maintained for three generations, but unfortunately these birds eventually died out.

SHORT-TAILED PARROT FINCH, FIJI RED-HEADED PARROT FINCH *Erythrura cyaneovirens* Peale

1

2

3

1. Chestnut-breasted finch, *Lonchura castaneothorax* 2. Java munia, *L. malacca ferruginosa*; 3. Three-colored mannikin, *L. malacca malacca;* 4. Royal parrot-finch, *Erythrura cyaneovirens;* 5. White and black-headed nun.

4

5

This species exists as several distinct races, of which presumably only two were ever imported.

Peale's Parrot Finch, *E.c. pealii* Hartl.

Forehead, crown of head, sides bright red; ear-coverts, chin and throat black; hind-neck, back and wing-coverts green; tail-coverts red, median tail feathers dull red, remainder black; upper breast blue, remainder of under-surface greenish blue; eyes brown; beak black; legs and feet yellowish. Total length about 11 cm.

Males can be recognized by their distinct trill call; other than that the sexes are hardly distinguishable.

Distribution: Fiji islands.

This subspecies was imported into Europe at the turn of the century; after that it appeared only rarely. In 1960 a larger shipment of these birds was sent to Dr. Burkhard in Switzerland. The requirements for this species are the same as for the red-headed parrot finch. In an aviary it breeds well and often produces several successive clutches. Free-standing nests are rarely built; instead this bird seems to prefer nest boxes. A clutch consists of two to four eggs, which are incubated for 13 days.

Royal Parrot Finch, *E.c. regia* Scl.

Adult male: Head scarlet red; back, wing-coverts and abdomen blue; lower back and rump dark green; upper tail-coverts red; central tail-feathers dull red, the remainder dark brown; eyes brown; beak black; legs and feet yellowish.

Adult female: The over-all blue coloration tends to be more greenish. Females older than 20 months are indistinguishable from males. Males are recognized by their trill call, which is identical to that given off by the red-headed parrot finch.

Distribution: New Hebrides and Banks Islands.

Royal Parrot Finches are difficult to adjust to captivity, since they are almost exclusively fruit eaters, and as such

116

they feed predominantly on the seeds of wild figs. Newly imported wild-caught birds must be given wild fig seeds, mixed with raisins and apples. Adjustment to grain feed is quite difficult. Among the seeds these birds tend to prefer canary seeds, which can be offered dry as well as germinated. They must also get oats and germinating wheat grains, apart from fruit. Animal protein should be offered in the form of fresh ant pupae and mealworms; egg food will also be eagerly taken by acclimated birds.

This species has been bred repeatedly, but breeding details have rarely been published. These birds build either free-standing nests in bushes or utilize a nest box. The nesting materials used are essentially the same as for other parrot finches. A clutch consists of three eggs. After the young have left the nest, they continue to be fed, mainly by the male, for another two to three weeks. They begin the molt after seven or eight weeks, and adult plumage is obtained after two to three months according to a Danish report. Royal parrot finches will breed repeatedly in quick succession.

Other Parrot Finches

Apart from those parrot finches already described in this book, three other species were shipped to Europe through the efforts of the collector M. Bregulla. He has also supplied different races of red-headed and blue-faced parrot finches, as well as short-tailed parrot finches. Collecting these birds and importing them was generously supported by Dr. R. Burkhard in Zurich, and he distributed some of these birds to various aviculturists and scientists. The information thus gathered about this genus has substantially increased our knowledge and understanding about parrot finches.

1

2

3

1. Red-eared parrot finch, *Erythrura coloria;* 2 and 3. Gouldian finch, *Chloebia gouldiae;* 4. Red-headed parrot finch, *Erythrura psittacea;* 5. Pintailed nonpareil, *Erythrura prasina.*

4

5

GREEN-TAILED PARROT FINCH, *Erythrura hyperythra* Reich.

Adult male: Lower forehead black; crown of head light blue; sides of head, throat and abdomen brown; breast and flanks green to bluish green, general color above green. Total length about 11 cm.

Adult female: Lower forehead washed grayish brown.

Distribution: Malaya, Java, Borneo, Celebes, Luzon, Lombok, Lesser Sunda Islands.

This species has never been bred in captivity.

GREEN-FACED PARROT FINCH, *Erythrura viridifacies* Delacour and Hachiuska

Adult male: General color above grass green; upper tail-coverts carmine red, the median tail-feathers are elongated and pointed, red; the remaining feathers blackish brown.

Adult female: General color above grass green, undersurface pale green; lower abdomen greenish yellow; upper tail-coverts red or red margined. Total length 13 to 14 cm.

Distribution: Luzon.

This species was discovered in 1920 in the vicinity of Manila. In 1935 one shipment with several hundred birds reached San Francisco. One specimen was used by Delacour and Hachisuka in 1936 to describe it as a new species.

Acclimating this species is not particularly difficult. According to Dr. Burkhard it is a pure seed eater, and insects and fruit are refused. In morphology and behavior this species resembles the closely related pintailed nonpareil. Dr. Burkhard describes this species as being 'definitely boring,' since it remains always rather timid. So far the green-faced parrot finch has never bred in captivity.

MANY-COLORED PARROT FINCH, *Erythrura coloria* Ripley & Rabor

Adult male: Forehead and sides of head cobalt-blue; at eye level bright red band crescent-shape along sides of neck downward to sides of breast. General color above dark green; lower back and upper tail-coverts red; median tail-feathers red, the remainder blackish brown with a red or greenish outer margin. Under-surface slightly lighter green; thigh ochre or yellow-ochre; eyes brown; beak black; legs and feet light brown. Total length about 10 cm.

Adult female: During the first year head colors blue and red, duller than in male of same age. In older birds the sexes cannot be distinguished on the basis of plumage (Prof. Ziswiler).

Distribution: Known only from Mount Katanglad in northern Mindanao (Philippines).

Through the efforts of Bregulla the first of these birds arrived in 1964 at Dr. Burkhard's in Zurich, who successfully acclimated and eventually bred them. Several pairs were distributed to other aviculturists. The following details on the care and maintenance of the newest and smallest of the parrot finches are based upon observations by Dr. Burkhard, as published in *Die Gefiederte Welt.*

These birds prefer primarily canary seed and stalks of spray millet for feed. Other varieties of millet are accepted only in small amounts. They will also readily feed on mealworms and fresh ant pupae, but they appear less interested in fruit. Food for rearing the young should consist of germinating canary seed, fresh and dried grass seeds, green food, ant pupae and boiled eggs (egg mixture). As per Dr. Burkhard's experiences, this species is one of the best breeders among parrot finches. The many-colored parrot finch prefers half-open nest boxes or horizontally placed parakeet boxes for nesting (similar to those used by the red-headed parrot finch). The nesting material used is grasses and coconut fibers; the nest is not lined with a soft cushioning material. A clutch has only one or two eggs, rarely three. After having left the nest, the young are still fed by their parents for another two weeks. After four or five

1
2
3

1 and 3. Red-headed parrot finch, *Erythrura psittacea;* 2. Three-colored parrot finch, *E. trichroa siglillifera;* 4 and 5. Pintailed nonpareil, *E. prasina.* All species are somewhat delicate when freshly imported and come up easily with intestinal and liver problems.

4

5

months adult plumage is complete.

The many-colored parrot finch is closely related to the red-headed parrot finch; behavior, vocalizing, the nest and nest-building and begging calls of the young are largely identical in both species. One can only hope that this beautiful species can be retained through an active breeding program, because it is doubtful whether there will ever be any additional imports coming in.

KLEINSCHMIDT'S PARROT FINCH, *Erythrura kleinschmidti* Fincsh

Forehead, fore-crown, bridle, ear-coverts and chin black; general colors above dark green; tail-coverts red; under-surface yellowish green. Total length about 10 cm.

Distribution: Viti Levu (Fiji Islands)

This species was first imported into Germany in 1914, together with Peale's parrot finch. One pair was shipped to the aviculturist Hugo Dicker in Halle (Germany). There is no further information available; other specimens have so far never been imported.

BLUE-GREEN PARROT FINCH, *Erythrura tricolor* Vieill

This species is very similar to the blue-faced parrot finch.
Distribution: Timor and Tanimbar Islands.

PAPUA PARROT FINCH, *Erythrura papuana* Hart

This species strongly resembles the blue-faced parrot finch. It is, however, substantially larger and has a stouter beak.

The Gouldian finch is very sensitive to drafts, but once acclimated it will become hardy and live for a long time.

124